Nutshells

Land Law

SECOND EDITION

Round Hall's Nutshell, Nutcase, Exam Focus and Legal Skills Series

NUTSHELL TITLES

Specially written for students of Irish law, each title in the Nutshell series from Round Hall is an accessible review of key principles, concepts and cases. Nutshells are both the ideal introductory text, and the perfect revision aid.

- Criminal Law – 2nd edition by Cecilia Ní Choileáin
- Tort – 2nd edition by Ursula Connolly
- Company Law – 2nd edition by Catherine McConville
- Constitutional Law – 2nd edition by Fergus Ryan
- The Irish Legal System by Dorothy Donovan
- Contract Law by Fergus Ryan
- Equity Law by Karl Dowling
- Family Law by Louise Crowley
- Employment Law by Dorothy Donovan
- Evidence by Ross Gorman

NUTCASE TITLES

Round Hall Nutcases are written to give you the key facts and principles of **important cases** in core legal subject areas. Straightforward, no-nonsense language makes Nutcases an easy way to understand and learn key cases.

- Tort – 2nd edition by Val Corbett
- Criminal Law by Majella Walsh
- Evidence by Neil Van Dokkum

EXAM FOCUS TITLES

The series is especially designed to support students in the weeks coming up to exams by providing a unique tutorial approach to answering questions.

- Criminal Law by Sarah Carew

LEGAL SKILLS TITLES

A new range of titles which help students master the essential skills needed in order to achieve success at both university and further career.

- How to Think, Write and Cite: Key Skills for Irish Law Students by Jennifer Schweppe, Rónán Kennedy, Elaine Fahey and Lawrence Donnelly

NUTSHELLS

Land Law

SECOND EDITION

by

Ruth Cannon
LLB (Dub), BCL (Oxon), BL

ROUND HALL   THOMSON REUTERS

Published in 2011 by
Thomson Reuters (Professional) Ireland Limited
(Registered in Ireland, Company No. 80867. Registered Office
and address for service 43 Fitzwilliam Place, Dublin 2)
trading as Round Hall

Typeset by Carrigboy Typesetting Services

Printed by Colourworld, Kilkenny, Ireland

ISBN 978-1-85800-593-5

A catalogue record for this book is available from the British Library.

Contents

Table of Cases vii
Table of Legislation xii

1 Introduction to Land Law and Equity **1**
    I.   The Land and Conveyancing Law Reform Act 2009 1
    II.   Interests in Land 2
    III.   Equity 3

2 Freehold Ownership **6**
    I.   Types of Freehold Ownership 6

3 Hybrid Interests **13**
    I.   Leases for Lives 13
    II.   Fee Farm Grants 14

4 Co-Ownership **16**
    I.   The Forms of Co-Ownership 16
    II.   Creation of a Joint Tenancy/Tenancy in Common 18
    III.   Severance of a Joint Tenancy 19
    IV.   Determination of Co-Ownership 20

5 Easements **21**
    I.   Characteristics of an Easement 21
    II.   Acquisition of Easements 25

6 Freehold Covenants **31**
    I.   Enforcement of post-December 2009 Freehold Covenants . . . 32
    II.   Enforcement of pre-December 2009 Freehold Covenants 32
    III.   Extinguishment of Freehold Covenants 38

7 Licences and Estoppel **40**
    I.   Types of Licences 40
    II.   Proprietary Estoppel 42

8 Leasehold Ownership **44**
    I.   Creation of a Landlord-Tenant Relationship 44
    II.   Types of Landlord-Tenant Relationships 47
    III.   Landlord-Tenant Relationships Falling within the
           Residential Tenancies Act 2004 48

IV.   Leasehold Arrangements Falling Outside the Residential
Tenancies Act 2004 54

9   Mortgages **64**
I.   Types of Mortgages 64
II.   Equity's Intervention in Relation to Mortgages 65
III.   Rights of a Mortgagor 69
IV.   Rights of a Mortgagee 69
V.   Rights of a Mortgagee under a pre-2009 Act Mortgage 69
VI.   Rights of a Mortgagee under a post-2009 Act Mortgage 72
VII.   Judgment Mortgages 74

10   Transfer of Land **75**
I.   Investigation of Title to Unregistered Land 76
II.   Investigation of Title to Registered Land 78
III.   The Family Home Protection Act 1976 83
IV.   The Civil Partnership and Certain Rights and
Obligations of Cohabitants Act 2010 87

11   Adverse Possession **88**
I.   Requirements for Adverse Possession 89
II.   Defences to Claims of Adverse Possession 101
III.   Effect of Extinguishment of Title 103
IV.   Special Situations of Adverse Possession 105

12   Succession Law **110**
I.   Wills 110
II.   Statutory Rights of Spouses/Civil Partners and Children
under the Succession Act 1965 119
III.   Intestacy 128
IV.   Rights of Cohabitants 131

Index 133

Table of Cases

IRELAND

A v C [2007] IEHC 120 96
ABC Deceased: XC, YC and ZC v RT, KU and JL, In the Estate of,
        unreported, High Court, Kearns J., April 2, 2003 125
Allied Irish Banks v Finnegan [1996] 1 I.L.R.M. 401 .... 85, 86

Bank of Ireland v Hanrahan, unreported, High Court, O'Hanlon J.,
        February 10, 1987 84
Bank of Ireland v Lady Lisa Ireland Ltd [1993] I.L.R.M. 235 59
Bank of Ireland v Smyth [1993] 2 I.R. 102 .... 85, 86
Batelle v Pinemeadow [2002] IEHC 120 .... 95, 97
Blackall v Blackall, unreported, High Court, McCracken J., June 28, 1996;
        unreported, Supreme Court, April 1, 1998 111
Bracken v Byrne, unreported, High Court, Clarke J., March 11, 2005 43
Browne v Fahy, unreported, High Court, Kenny J., October 24, 1975 90
Browne v Ryan [1901] 2 I.R. 653 67
Byrne v Byrne, unreported, High Court, January 18, 1980 19

Campus and Stadium Development v Dublin Waterworld [2005] IEHC 334 59
Canty v Private Residential Tenancies Board, High Court, Laffoy J.,
        August 8, 2007 52
C.C. v W.C. [1990] 2 I.R. 143 122
Containercare (Ireland) Ltd v Wycherly [1982] I.R. 413 19
Convey v Regan [1952] I.R. 56 97
Collins, Re: O'Connell v Bank of Ireland [1998] 2 I.R. 596 118
Cork Corporation v Lynch [1995] 2 I.L.R.M. 598 ....100, 101
Craig v Greer [1899] 1 I.R. 258 58
Cregan and Another v Taviri Ltd, High Court, Charleton J., May 30, 2008 56
Cue Club Ltd v Navaro Ltd, unreported, Supreme Court, Murphy J.,
        October 23, 1996 59
Curtin Deceased, Re [1991] 2 I.R. 562 118

Doyle v O'Neill, unreported, High Court, O'Hanlon J., January 13, 1995 .... 92, 95, 99
Drohan v Drohan [1984] I.L.R.M. 179 107
DS v KM, unreported, High Court, Carroll J., December 19, 2003 123
Dundalk UDC v Conway, unreported, High Court, Blayney J.,
        December 15, 1987 91
Dunne v Iarnród Éireann [2007] IEHC 314 .... 93, 94, 95, 100
Dunnes Stores (Ilac Centre) Ltd v Irish Life Assurance PLC [2008] IEHC 114 57
Durack (Seamus) Manufacturing v Considine [1987] I.R. 677 .... 99, 100

Dwyer Nolan Developments Ltd v Kingscroft Developments Ltd
[1999] 1 I.L.R.M. 141 .... 26, 27

F v JDF, unreported, Supreme Court, McGuinness J., July 12, 2005;
[2005] IESC 45 43
Feehan v Leamy [2000] IEHC 118 .... 91, 98, 100

Genport Ltd v Crofter Properties Ltd, High Court, McGovern J.,
February 20, 2008 62
Gleeson v Feehan [1991] I.L.R.M. 783 107
Gleeson v Purcell [1997] I.L.R.M. 522 109
Glynn, Re [1990] 2 I.R. 326 112
G.M., Re (1972) 106 I.L.T.R. 82 121
Governors of National Maternity Hospital, Dublin v McGouran
[1994] 1 I.L.R.M. 521 45
Greene Property v Shalaine Modes [1978] 1 I.L.R.M. 222 57
Griffin v Bleithin [1999] 2 I.L.R.M. 182 .... 23, 93, 99
Groome v Fodhla Printing Co. Ltd [1943] I.R. 380 55
Guckian v Brennan [1981] I.R. 478 82

Hamilton v Hamilton [1982] I.R. 466 86
Hanna v Pollock [1900] 2 I.R. 664 22

Irish Shell v Costello [1981] I.L.R.M. 66 44–46

Jameson v Squire [1948] I.R. 153 47
Johnston v Smith [1896] I.R. 83 102
Julian, Re [1950] I.R. 57 116–118

K.C. v C.F.; M.C., unreported, High Court, Carroll J., December 16, 2003 124
Kieran, In b. [1933] I.R. 22 112
Kenny Homes v Leonard, unreported, Supreme Court, Lynch J.,
June 18, 1998 46

L.B.; E.B. v S.S., Re [1998] 2 I.L.R.M. 141 122
Lindsay v Tomlinson, unreported, High Court, Carroll J., February 13, 1996 118
Lynch v Burke, unreported, High Court, McCracken J., July 30, 1999 ..... 118, 119
Lynch v Dolan [1973] I.R. 319 61

McCausland v Murphy (1881) 9 L.R. Ir. 9 47
McDonald v Norris [1999] 1 I.L.R.M. 270 (HC): [2000] 1 I.L.R.M. 382 (SC) 122, 123
McLoughlin, In b. [1936] I.R. 223 112
Meagher & Or v Luke J. Healy Pharmacy Limited [2010] IEHC 40 56
Middleton v Clarence (1877) 11 I.R.C.L. 499 23
Moley v Fee [2007] IEHC 143 91

LAND LAW

Moorehead v Tiilikainen [1999] 2 I.L.R.M. 471 116
Mulhern v Brady [2001] IEHC 23 90
Murphy v Murphy [1980] I.R. 183 . . . . 89, 97

Nestor v Murphy [1979] I.R. 326 85

O'Connor v Foley [1906] 1 I.R. 20 104
O'Donnell v O'Donnell, unreported, High Court, Kelly J., March 24, 1999 111
O'Dwyer v Keegan [1997] 2 I.L.R.M. 401 120
Ó Siodhachain v O'Mahony, unreported, High Court, Kearns J.,
    October 31, 2002 45

Perry v Woodfarm Homes Ltd [1975] I.R. 104 104–105

Rankin v McMurtry (1889) 24 L.T.R. Ir. 290 104
Redfont Ltd v Custom House Dock Management Ltd, unreported, High Court,
    Shanley J., March 31, 1998 24
Rice v Dublin Corporation [1947] I.R. 425 56
Rowe v Law [1978] I.R. 55 . . . . 117, 118

Smith v Irish Rail, unreported, High Court, Peart J., October 9, 2002 . . . . 45, 46
Smith v Savage [1906] 1 I.R. 469 108
Smyth v Halpin, unreported, High Court, Geoghegan J.,
    December 20, 1996 . . . . 42, 43
Somers v Weir [1979] I.R. 94 85
Start Mortgages v Gunn, unreported, High Court, Dunne J., July 29, 2011 70

Tracey Enterprises MacAdam Limited v Drury [2006] IEHC 381 . . . . 93, 98
Treacy v Dublin Corporation [1993] 1 I.R. 305 24

Údarás na Gaeltachta v Uisce Glan Teoranta, High Court, O'Neill J.,
    March 13, 2007; [2007] IEHC 95 55

Vaughan v Cottingham [1961] I.R. 184 108

Wanze Properties (Ireland) Ltd v Mastertron Ltd [1992] I.L.R.M. 746 57
Whelan v Madigan [1978] I.L.R.M. 136 55
Whipp v Mackey [1927] I.R. 372 . . . . 41, 59
William Bennett Construction Limited v Greene, unreported, Supreme Court,
    Keane C.J., February 25, 2004; [2004] IESC 15 43
Wright v Tracey (1874) 8 I.R.C.L. 478 46

TABLE OF CASES

ENGLAND

Ashburn Anstalt v Arnold [1989] Ch. 1 41

Ballard's Conveyance, Re [1937] Ch. 473 36
Baxter v Four Oaks Properties Ltd [1965] Ch. 816 38
Bernays v Prosser [1963] 2 All E.R. 321 47
Biggs v Hoddinott [1898] 2 Ch. 307 68
Bradley v Carritt [1903] A.C. 253 67
Bravda, Re [1968] 1 W.L.R. 479 113

Cityland Property (Holdings) Ltd v Dabrah [1968] Ch. 166 68
Cook, In b. [1960] 1 W.L.R. 353 112
Copeland v Greenhalf [1952] Ch. 488 23

Dalton v Angus & Co (1881) 6 App. Cas. 740 23
Doe d Curzon v Edmonds (1840) 6 M. & W. 295 102
Dolphin's Conveyance, Re [1970] Ch. 654 38
Dyce v Hay (1852) 1 Macq. 305 23

Edginton v Clark [1964] 1 Q.B. 367 102

Fairclough v Swan Brewery Co. Ltd [1912] A.C. 565 66
Fairweather v St Marylebone Property Co. Ltd [1963] A.C. 510 105
Fourmaids Ltd v Dudley Marshall (Properties) Ltd [1957] Ch. 317 70

Hill v Tupper (1863) 2 H. & C. 121 22
Hughes v Griffin [1969] 1 W.L.R. 1295 96
Hunt v Luck [1902] I Ch. 428 77

Inwards v Baker [1965] 2 Q.B. 29 42

J.A. Pye (Oxford) Limited [2002] UKHL 30 91

King v Smith [1950] 1 All E.R. 553 107

Kingsnorth Finance v Tizard [1996] 1 W.L.R. 783 82
Krelinger v New Properties Meat and Cold Storage Co. Ltd [1914] A.C. 25 67

Lace v Chantler [1944] 1 All E.R. 305 46
Leigh v Jack (1879) 5 Ex. D. 264 .... 91, 99, 100

Malayan Credit v Jack Chia-MPH Ltd [1986] A.C. 549 18
Moody v Steggles (1879) 12 Ch D 261 22
Multiservice Bookbinding Ltd v Marden [1979] Ch. 84 68

National Provincial Bank v Ainsworth [1965] A.C. 1175 82
Noakes & Co. Ltd v Rice [1902] A.C. 24 .... 66, 67

Ofulue v Bossert [2008] EWCA Civ 7 102

Peckham v Ellison [1999] Conv. 353 27
Phipps v Pears [1965] 1 Q.B. 76 24
Powell v McFarlane [1979] 38 P. & C.R. 452 92
Purefoy v Rodgers (1671) 2 Wns Saun 380, 84 E.R. 1101 9

Renals v Cowlishaw (1878) 9 Ch D 125 36
Rhone v Stephens [1994] 2 A.C. 310 34
Rogers v Hosegood [1900] 2 Ch. 388 36

Street v Mountford [1985] A.C. 809 46

Tichborne v Weir (1892) 67 L.T. 735 104
The Lord Advocate v Lord Lovat (1880) 5 App. Cas. 273 92
Thorn v Dickens [1906] W.N. 54 116
Tulk v Moxhay (1848) 2 Ph. 774 .... 34–36, 38

Union of London and Smith's Bank Ltd's Conveyance, Re [1933] Ch. 611 37

Walcite Ltd v Ferrishurst Ltd [1999] 1 All E.R. 977 82
Walsh v Lonsdale (1882) 21 Ch D 9 47
Webb v Pollmount Ltd [1966] Ch. 584 82
Wheeldon v Burrows (1879) 12 Ch D 31 .... 27, 28
Whitby v Mitchell (1890) 44 Ch D 85 9
Williams & Glyns Bank v Boland [1981] A.C. 487 82
Williams v Hensman (1861) 1 J. & H. 546 19
Winter Garden Theatre (London) Ltd v Millennium Productions Ltd
    [1948] A.C. 173 41
Wright v Macadam [1949] 2 K.B. 744 23

Northern Ireland

Fulton v Kee [1961] N.I. 1 112

Table of Legislation

IRELAND

PRE-1922 STATUTES

Conveyancing Act 1881 . . . . 71, 73
    s.6 28
    s.14 . . . . 58, 59
    s.19 71
    s.19(1)(i) 71, 73
    s.20 71
    s.58 37
Conveyancing Act 1911
    s.4 73
Conveyancing Acts 1881–1911 73
Fines and Recoveries Act 1834 . . . . 8, 9
Forfeiture Act 1870 103
Judgment Mortgage (Ireland) Act 1850
    s.4 74
Judgment Mortgage (Ireland) Acts 1850–1858 74
Landlord and Tenant (Amendment) (Ireland) Act 1860
    ("Deasy's Act") 14, 44–48, 54
    s.3 . . . . 44, 45
    s.7 58
    s.40 58
    s.42 . . . . 54, 55
    s.52 60
Law of Property (Amendment) Act 1860
    s.13 108
Partition Acts 1868–76 20
Prescription Act 1832 29
    s.1 29
Prescription (Ireland) Act 1858 29
Quia Emptores 1290 14
Real Property Limitation Act 1833 88
Renewable Leasehold Conversion Act 1849 14
Settled Land Act 1882 . . . . 11, 12
Settled Land Acts 1882–1890 . . . . 10, 11
Supreme Court of Judicature (Ireland) Act 1877 4

Post–1922 Statutes

Administration of Estates Act 1959 108
British-Irish Agreement Act 1999 89
Civil Law (Miscellaneous Provisions) Act 2008 1
    s.47 62
Civil Law (Miscellaneous Provisions) Act 2011 1
    s.38 30
    s.57 29
Civil Partnership and Certain Rights and Obligations of Cohabitants
    Act 2010 .... 1, 87, 119, 131, 132
    Pt 4 .... 83, 87
    s.29 87
    s.70 121
    s.73 .... 129, 130
    s.81 119
    s.86 .... 120, 121
    s.111 131
    s.194 132
    s.194(5) 132
Family Home Protection Act 1976 .... 75, 82–86, 87
    s.3(1) 86, 87
    s.4 86
Family Law Act 1995 85
    s.54 87
    s.54(1)(a) 84
    s.54(1)(b) 84, 87
Housing (Miscellaneous Provisions) Act 2009
    s.100 48
Housing (Private Rented Dwellings) Act 1982 .... 49, 63
Interpretation Act 2005
    s.27 .... 70, 71
Land and Conveyancing Law Reform Act 2009 .... 1, 5, 8–10, 11, 12,
                    13, 15, 27–30, 32, 64, 65, 69–72, 74, 75, 78
    Pt 4 .... 10, 11, 12
    Pt 11 74
    s.9 14
    s.9(3) 14
    s.11 .... 7, 11
    s.11(1) 10
    s.11(2) 10
    s.11(3) 10
    s.12 .... 15, 48
    s.13 9
    s.14 13

s.16 9
s.17 9
s.18(9) 11
s.19 11
s.19(1)(a)(i) 11
s.19(1)(a)(ii) 11
s.19(1)(b) 11
s.20(1) 12
s.21 12
s.21(4) 12
s.21(2)(a) 12
s.21(2)(b) 12
s.22 12
s.22(3) 12
s.30 .... 19, 20
s.31 .... 19, 20, 74
ss.34–37 29
s.35 29
s.35(2) 30
s.35(3) 30
s.36 30
s.36(1) 30
s.37 29
s.38 30
s.39 30
s.40 28
s.49 .... 32, 39
s.49(6)(b) 32
s.50 .... 38, 39
s.50(2) 39
s.56 76
s.67 75
s.89 64
ss.97–111 72
s.97 72
s.97(2) 72
s.98 72
s.99 72
s.100 .... 72, 73
s.100(1) 73
s.100(2) 73
s.100(3) 72, 73
s.100(4) 72
s.100(5) 72
s.100(6) 72

s.101(1) 72
s.101(2) 73
s.101(3) 73
s.102 73
s.108 73
s.108(1) 73
s.115 74
s.115(a) 74
s.116 .... 74, 76
s.116(3)(a) 74
s.116(3)(b) 74
s.117 74
s.132 .... 1, 54
Landlord and Tenant (Amendment) Act 1971 63
Landlord and Tenant (Amendment) Act 1980 .... 48, 54, 55, 62
Pt II 61–63
Pt III 63
Pt IV 61–63
s.17 .... 61, 62
s.17(1) 61, 62
s.17(2) 62
ss.65–88 .... 54, 61
s.65 .... 55, 56
s.65(2) 55, 56
s.65(3) 55, 56
s.66 56
s.67 56
s.74 14
Landlord and Tenant (Ground Rents) Acts 1967–2005 .... 49, 59, 62
Landlord and Tenant (Ground Rents)(No. 2) Act 1978 62
s.9 .... 62, 63
s.10 62
s.10, Conditions 3–7 63
s.15 62
s.16 63
s.27 59
Registration of Deeds and Titles Act 2006 .... 1, 13, 78
s.50(d) 106
Registration of Title Act 1964 .... 13, 64, 65, 78, 105, 106
s.3 106
s.24 79
s.32 83
s.62(7) 70
s.69(1) 81
s.72 79

TABLE OF LEGISLATION

s.72(1) 79, 81
s.72(1)(j) 79, 82
Residential Tenancies Act 2004 .... 1, 48–50, 53, 54, 63
   Pt 2 49
   Pt 4 50–54
   Pt 5 51
   Pt 6 .... 49, 52
   s.3(2) 48
   s.12 49
   s.16 50
   s.28(2) 50, 51
   s.33 .... 53, 54
   s.34 .... 50, 52, 53
   s.34, Condition 1 53
   s.40 51
   s.42(1) 51
   s.58(3) 53
   s.62 51
   s.65(4) 52
   s.66 52
   ss.66–68 52
   s.66, Table 1 53
   s.66, Table 2 53
   s.67 .... 51, 52
   s.67(3) 52
   s.68 53
   s.182 49
   s.186 50
   s.192 63
Statute of Frauds 47
Statute of Limitations 1957 .... 3, 57, 82, 88, 89, 101, 102, 104, 109
   s.13(1) 88
   s.13(2) 88
   s.13(2)(a) 107, 108
   s.14(1) 89
   s.17 106
   s.17(1) 96
   s.17(2) 106
   s.18 89
   s.18(1) 89, 90
   s.24 88
   s.48 103
   s.48(2) 103
   s.49 103
   s.49(1)(a) 103

s.51 101
s.58 101
s.71(1) 102
s.71(2) 102
Succession Act 1965 .... 3, 107, 108, 109, 110, 111, 112, 113, 115,
                                                  117, 119, 120, 131
   Pt IX 110
   s.30(4) 12
   s.56 121
   s.71(2) 130
   s.90 .... 117, 118, 119
   s.98 116
   s.111 .... 107, 119
   s.117 .... 120–123, 124, 125, 126, 131
   s.121 119
   s.125 108
   s.125(1) 109
   s.125(2) 109
   s.126 .... 107, 108

Introduction to Land Law and Equity

There are a number of purposes behind this book. The first is to provide the beginner in land law with an outline knowledge of the subject. Secondly, the book aims to assist the student who has covered a number of topics in land law quite well, but is uncertain as to how these topics fit into the general structure of the subject. The third purpose of the book is to help those who are preparing for exams and are under pressure to cover the important material quickly.

This introductory chapter begins by giving an outline of a typical Irish land law course. It then discusses the various sources of land law. There are three main sources of land law: the common law, equity and statute law. Students often find it difficult to understand the way in which these diverse sources interact with one another. In particular, comprehension of the role played by the courts of equity may be problematic. Evidence of the huge impact equity has had on land law is to be found throughout the course. For this reason, the role of equity in land law is also summarised in this introductory chapter.

I. THE LAND AND CONVEYANCING LAW REFORM ACT 2009

All students of Irish land law today need to be fully aware of recent legislative changes, the most important of which is the Land and Conveyancing Law Reform Act 2009 (the "2009 Act"), the provisions of which (excluding s.132, relating to upwards-only rent review clauses) came into effect on December 1, 2009—*the* key date from point of view of Irish land law.

The 2009 Act, which effects important changes to almost every area of Irish land law (other than adverse possession and, to a lesser degree, leasehold ownership), is dealt with on a chapter-by-chapter basis in this book. Ignore it at your peril.

Other recent statutes which have been enacted since the first edition of this text include the Residential Tenancies Act 2004, the Registration of Deeds and Titles Act 2006 and the Civil Partnership and Certain Rights and Obligations of Cohabitants Act 2010. Changes have also been effected to landlord and tenant law by the Civil Law (Miscellaneous Provisions) Act 2008 and to easements by the Civil Law (Miscellaneous Provisions) Act 2011.

II. Interests in Land

Lawyers normally refer to rights over land as *interests in land*. There are a number of different interests in land (see Chapters 2–9).

Freehold ownership

First of all, we need to discuss what is meant by ownership of land. Ownership is generally understood by the non-lawyer to be the right to permanent exclusive possession of land, the owner having the right to dispose of it to whoever he wishes, either during his lifetime or by will. In practice, matters are not so simple, since land law recognises different types of ownership. The above situation describes the fee simple freehold owner.

Generally speaking, a freehold owner is someone who has the exclusive right to possession of land with no landlord above him. However, not all freehold owners have the right to exclusive possession of the land forever. There are other freehold owners, such as the holder of a life estate, whose freehold interest determines on their death. These individuals do not have the right to freely transfer the land, nor may they leave it by will.

Leasehold ownership

In addition, a tenant under a lease is also described by land law as the owner of land. Although he is not the freehold owner, he has what is known as a leasehold ownership, i.e. the right to exclusive possession of the land according to the terms of his agreement with the landlord.

Licensees

In contrast to leasehold ownership, a licence over land is a mere permission from the owner of land to occupy it. There is no agreement between the owner (licensor) and occupier (licensee) to hold as landlord and tenant. A licence is merely a personal right and this creates problems for the licensee when the owner of the land over which the licence subsists sells on the land to a third party.

Easements

The term "easement" is used to describe a limited right to carry out a particular act on a neighbour's land or, in some cases, to prevent him from doing a particular act on his land. Easements may be positive or negative. An example of a positive easement would be a right to cross a defined path on a neighbour's land to get to a main road. A right, held by a landowner, to stop a neighbour building on his own land, on the ground that it reduces the level of light coming through the windows of the landowner's house, constitutes a negative easement.

FREEHOLD COVENANTS

Additionally, the device of freehold covenants gives a limited right of control over one's neighbour by requiring him to do or, more usually, refrain from doing, a particular act. A may enter into a covenant with B whereby B promises not to build on B's land. A has the benefit of the covenant, namely the right to sue if B breaches his promise. Moreover, future owners of A's land may be able to enforce the covenant against future owners of B's land.

ACQUIRING INTERESTS IN LAND

Freehold ownership of land may be transferred inter vivos or on death. A transfer inter vivos is a transfer from someone who is still alive at the time of the transfer. Inter vivos transfers may be either sales or voluntary convey-ances, namely gifts. Mortgages are subject to special rules and are dealt with later in this book. Transfer on death may occur by will or, if there is no valid will, according to the rules of intestacy, and is regulated by the Succession Act 1965. The rules for creation and transfer of leases, easements, and rights under covenants are dealt with in the chapters on these topics. De facto ownership of land may also be acquired by adverse possession of the land for the period laid down in the Statute of Limitations 1957.

III. EQUITY

Having briefly summarised the topics covered in this text, it is now proposed to consider the important historical concept of equity and the role it plays in our modern land law system.

WHAT IS EQUITY?

The term equity is used to refer to the legal rules and concepts developed by the courts of chancery as opposed to the common law courts. The original basis for our land law is the common law, as developed by the common law courts. However, in the late Middle Ages, the rival courts of equity/chancery were developed. They introduced changes in the law, modifying the common law to some extent. Because the courts of equity co-existed with the common law courts, there was initial rivalry between the two courts. This culminated in an attempt by the common law courts to deny the validity of the rules of equity. However, the seventeenth century political situation led to the courts of equity being assigned superiority over those of the common law. Thereafter, the common law courts could not nullify the modifications introduced by equity. There remained, however, some procedural difficulties for the litigant who wished to rely on equitable rules. To invoke a common law principle, it was necessary to apply to the common law courts, whereas those who wished to rely on an equitable rule had to go to the courts of equity. This led to expense and delay in litigation. This was remedied by the Supreme Court of Judicature (Ireland) Act 1877. The position today is that a single court, the High Court, has the responsibility of administering the rules of the common law, subject to the modifications introduced by equity and statute law.

EQUITABLE INTERESTS

The most important change introduced by equity was the development of equitable interests. These were interests in land which were not regarded as valid by the common law courts, but which equity felt should be recognised. They are to be contrasted with legal interests, namely rights which were recognised and enforced at common law.

Equitable interests include the interest of a beneficiary under a trust and the right to claim an interest in land under the equitable doctrine of estoppel, together with certain mortgages and leases which do not satisfy the common law formalities for the creation of such interests, but which equity feels should be recognised nonetheless.

Equitable interests are weaker than common law or "legal" interests in one respect. They will be extinguished if unregistered land over which they subsist comes into the hands of a purchaser of the legal estate for value without notice. (For a definition of this privileged person, who is commonly known as *equity's darling*, see Chapter 10: Transfer of Land.) Equity feels that it would be unjust for such an individual to be bound by equitable interests.

Finally, equity recognises rights to set aside a transaction for undue influence, mistake or misrepresentation in situations where the common law does not. We call these particular rights "mere equities" because they are not as strong in nature as the equitable interests mentioned above, losing priority to them in cases of conflict.

THE TRUST

The trust is the most important of all equitable interests. Put simply, it is a concept whereby an individual known as a trustee holds legal title to land for the benefit of another individual known as a beneficiary. The trustee cannot profit from his dealings with the trust property, even though he is the legal owner of it. Only the beneficiary is allowed to take a substantive benefit from the trust property. In practical terms, the beneficiary is the real owner of the property: even though he is not recognised as the owner at common law, equity treats him as the equitable owner. In some cases, the equitable rights of the beneficiary may even extend to compelling the trustee to transfer to him the legal title to the property.

Describing someone as being the equitable owner of property or as owning an equitable estate in property means the same thing. Basically, these terms refer to the fact that the legal owner of the property in question holds it on trust for that person, and is not allowed to draw a benefit from it for himself. The creation of a trust separates the legal and equitable estates in the property. The trustee, as the legal owner, has common law rights over the property but equity requires him to exercise his common law rights for the benefit of the beneficiary, who is therefore known as the equitable owner. In contrast, if no trust exists in relation to property, the common law owner is the absolute owner and is not curtailed by equity from exercising his common law rights.

A trust of property can be created either expressly or impliedly. An express trust is created either when the owner of property expressly declares himself trustee of it for the benefit of someone else or, alternatively, when he conveys it to a third party to hold as trustee for the benefit of that person. In other words, an express trust is one which is intentionally created by the grantor of the land. Sometimes, express trusts are created for tax avoidance purposes, or because the beneficiary under the trust is a minor and incapable of managing the gift, or perhaps because the settlor is afraid that the beneficiary will dissipate the property if given legal title to it.

There are also a number of situations where trusts will be implied by the courts. For example, if an individual buys property in someone else's name, or makes a gift of his property to another person, equity presumes a resulting trust in his favour. He is presumed not to intend to give his property away without receiving a benefit in return. What happens in this situation is that the legal ownership in the property passes to the recipient of the gift, who is regarded as holding the gift on trust for the person making the gift. This kind of implied trust is known as a resulting trust because the gift effectively results back to the grantor. The presumption of resulting trust can be rebutted by evidence of an intention on the part of the grantor that the recipient should have absolute title to the property.

Equity also implies constructive trusts in a number of miscellaneous situations in order to meet the demands of justice.

The category of implied trust has been recently extended by the new statutory trust implied by the Land and Conveyancing Law Reform Act 2009 in the case of properties held under life estates or estates *pur autre vie*.

2

Freehold Ownership

I. TYPES OF FREEHOLD OWNERSHIP

There are four types of freehold ownership, known as the four freehold estates:

- The fee simple
- The fee tail
- The life estate
- The estate *pur autre vie*

i) THE FEE SIMPLE

The first and most powerful form of freehold ownership is the fee simple. The word "fee" is a reference to "forever". The added word "simple" means "without qualification". The owner of a standard fee simple (the "fee simple absolute") estate has the right to ownership of the relevant land forever. He is the absolute owner of the land.

However, there are two modified fee simple estates which are not quite equivalent to absolute ownership. These are the determinable fee simple and the fee simple subject to a condition.

The determinable fee simple is a fee simple estate which will end automatically on the happening of a specified event, which may or may not happen; an example would be "to Mary in fee simple, until she marries". Although the estate might not go on forever, it is described as a fee simple, albeit a modified one, because it has the potential to go on forever if the event in question, in this case Mary's marriage, does not occur. If the event occurs, the estate will revert back automatically to the person who granted the determinable fee. His interest is known as a possibility of reverter.

The second type of modified fee simple is the fee simple upon a condition, which has also been called a conditional fee simple; an example would be "to Mary on condition that she does not marry". Again, this may come to an end if the specified condition or event occurs and the grantor, or the person specified to get the fee simple on occurrence of the condition, exercises the right of entry onto the property. The distinction between a conditional and a determinable fee is that with a conditional fee, the mere happening of the event (Mary's marriage) will not automatically cause the estate to end. It merely gives the grantor the gift over a right of entry and the estate only terminates on the exercise of this right.

When faced with a grant of a modified fee simple, in order to decide whether it is a conditional or determinable fee, it is necessary to look at the words used in the grant. Certain words are regarded as giving rise to a determinable fee simple and others are regarded as giving rise to a conditional fee simple.

Words such as "while", "during", "as long as" and "until", if included in the grant of a modified fee, signify a determinable fee simple, whereas words such as "on condition that", "provided that" and "but if" create a fee simple upon a condition.

Sometimes there may be an attempted grant of a modified fee which may fail because the imposition of the condition or determining event is inconsistent with the nature of a fee simple or contrary to public policy or constitutional principles.

If the grant is one of a determinable fee and the imposition of the determining event is objectionable, the whole gift fails. The grantee gets nothing. However, if the condition in a conditional fee is impermissible, the condition will be severed from the rest of the grant and struck down, the result being that the grantee obtains an absolute fee simple. This is another important difference between determinable fee simples and fee simples upon a condition.

The following is a list of potentially impermissible restrictions on modified fees:

- restrictions on alienation;
- restrictions on residence;
- name and arms clauses;
- restrictions on marriage;
- ethnic, sectarian and religious restrictions.

Under s.11 of the Land and Conveyancing Law Reform Act 2009 (the "2009 Act") the absolute or modified fee simple is the only freehold estate that can subsist at law after December 1, 2009. All other freehold estates (to the extent that they survive at all) exist in equity only, behind a trust.

ii) THE FEE TAIL

The significance of the fee tail estate has been greatly reduced by the 2009 Act. Most fee tail estates have been converted into fee simple estates under s.13 of the 2009 Act and only a very small number survive.

The fee tail was a lesser estate than the fee simple because it did not confer absolute ownership. Where land was given to an individual in fee tail, this meant that that person had the use of the land for their life but that on their death it would automatically pass to their descendants according to the rules of primogeniture. The same process was repeated in subsequent generations, with the fee tail only ending if all the blood descendants of the original tenant in tail died out.

In the meantime, the land subject to the fee tail was completely inalienable. All that any tenant in tail could sell was their life estate in the land. This meant that a purchaser from that person would merely get an estate *pur autre vie*, i.e. an estate lasting until the death of the person currently entitled under the fee tail. This was a very uncertain interest and it is not surprising that land subject to a fee tail was virtually impossible to alienate.

The Fines and Recoveries Act 1834 (the "1834 Act") represented a milestone, since it laid down a relatively simple and clearly defined mechanism for converting a fee tail into a fee simple. A present or future tenant in tail could achieve this result by executing a disentailing assurance and enrolling it in the Central Office of the High Court within six months of its execution. The one drawback was that the tenant in tail had to get the consent of an individual known as the protector of the settlement, usually a person or persons named in the document creating the fee tail as such.

If the tenant in tail failed to get the consent of the protector of the settlement, he was left with a base fee. A base fee extinguished the claims of the descendants of the tenant in tail, but did not extinguish the claims of those entitled to the property should the descendants of the tenant in tail ever die out.

If the tenant in tail made an even greater mistake and failed to enroll the disentailing assurance in the High Court in time, he was then left with a lesser interest still, a voidable base fee. Not only did this estate not bar the claims of remaindermen, but it also allowed the issue in tail to enter on the land at any time and revive the fee tail.

The usual form of fee tail, which provided for descent according to the rules of primogeniture, was known as a fee tail general. However, there were also specialised types of fee tail which could be created, for example a fee tail male or female confined to descendants of a particular gender, or a fee tail under which only descendants of a particular couple could inherit. Specialised fee tails could be barred under the 1834 Act in exactly the same way as general fee tails.

The 1834 Act was repealed by the 2009 Act which effectively abolished the fee tail estate.

Section 13 of the 2009 Act provides that any attempt to create a fee tail after the coming into effect of the Act on December 1, 2009 will instead create a fee simple. In addition, all fee tails (including base fees and voidable base fees) in existence at the coming into effect of the 2009 Act (with two exceptions) shall henceforth be regarded as fee simple estates.

The only fee tails which will survive the coming into effect of the 2009 Act are:

- fee tails subject to a protectorship, which are excluded from the operation of s.13 for the duration of the protectorship;
- fee tails with possibility of issue extinct, for example, where the fee tail is for the descendants of a particular couple, one of whom is already deceased without issue.

Neither category is likely to long survive the coming into effect of the 2009 Act.

iii) THE LIFE ESTATE/ESTATE *PUR AUTRE VIE*

The owner of a life estate only has an estate in the land for his life. The owner of an estate *pur autre vie* is in the same position as the holder of a life estate, only weaker. The continuance of his estate is dependent on the continuance of the life of another person.

Estates *pur autre vie* and life estates are limited in duration and one issue which arises is what happens to the property after these estates come to an end. If no one is specified as getting the property after the estate ends, then it automatically reverts to the grantor in fee simple (or, if he is deceased, his estate). This is known as a reversion. Alternatively, the document creating the relevant estate may name a third party as entitled to the property after the estate ends. This is known as a remainder.

Traditionally, the law acted so as to impose restrictions on the type of remainders which could be created in favour of third parties. There were a large number of rather complex rules limiting the circumstances in which such interests could be created, such as the rule against perpetuities, the common law remainder rules, the rule in *Whitby v Mitchell* ((1890) 44 Ch D 85) and the rule in *Purefoy v Rogers* ((1671) 2 Wns Saun 380, 84 E.R. 1101). Section 16 of the 2009 Act abolishes all of these rules, without qualification, so as to allow the unrestricted creation of remainders in favour of third parties.

Furthermore, s.17 makes clear that s.16 retrospectively validates future interests pre-dating the 2009 Act which would have previously been invalid under the above rules. However, such retrospective validation cannot apply where a person has already altered their position to their detriment in reliance on the invalidity of the interest.

The position of life estates and estates *pur autre vie* generally has also been significantly altered by the 2009 Act. First, their status has been reduced to that of equitable interests only.

Section 11(1) of the 2009 Act limits the categories of legal estates to those freehold and leasehold estates specified in subss.(2) and (3) of that section. The only freehold estate which now subsists at common law is the fee simple estate in possession (this term is defined in s.11(2) in such a way as to include determinable and conditional fee simples in possession).

Estates such as the life estate, the estate *pur autre vie* and fee simple reversions and remainders will henceforth exist in equity only, and the consequence of this is that they are subject to the Trusts of Land regime set out in Pt 4 of the 2009 Act.

Prior to the coming into effect of the 2009 Act, life estates and estates *pur autre vie* were subject to the Settled Land Acts regime laid down by the Settled Land Acts 1882–1890. Land held under a life estate/estate *pur autre vie* was land subject to a settlement and the life tenant/tenant *pur autre vie,* the tenant for life within the meaning of these Acts.

A tenant for life had the power to lease the land subject to certain limitations in relation to the duration of the lease and also had the power to sell same in fee simple (under the common law applicable prior to the Settled Land Acts, all that a life tenant or tenant *pur autre vie* could transfer was an estate *pur autre vie*). The rights of the remainderman or reversioner were not extinguished on such sale, but were transferred to the purchase money (capital money) received in respect of same by a process known as "overreaching".

It was a condition of this process that the capital money be paid by the purchaser directly to individuals known as trustees of the settlement, whose duty was to administer it according to the terms of the settlement. If the purchaser did not pay the capital money to at least two trustees he would not take the property free of the future interests. If he did so, however, he would get an absolute title to the property.

Determining the identity of the trustees of the settlement was a complex process, which involved asking a number of questions:

- Were there trustees under the original settlement with a power of sale/power to consent to a sale?
- If not, were there persons declared by the original settlement to be trustees of the settlement for the purposes of the Settled Land Acts?
- If not, were there persons with a power of sale of any other land comprised in the settlement apart from the land to be sold?
- If not, were there persons under the settlement with a future power of sale over the land?

If no one qualified under the above tests, then an application could be made to court for the appointment of trustees.

Under the Settled Land Acts regime, the role of the trustees of the settlement (who did not hold a legal interest in the property) was confined to receipt of the purchase money. The sale was effected by the tenant for life, and although the trustees had to be notified of the sale, the tenant for life did not have to go along with their wishes (except in the case of the sale of a principal mansion house, where the trustees had to give their consent).

The 2009 Act repeals the Settled Land Acts regime and replaces it with the new trusts of land regime set out in Pt 4 of the 2009 Act.

The provisions of Pt 4 apply to every kind of trust, whether an express holding trust, an express trust for sale, a resulting or constructive trust or the statutory implied trust arising under s.11 of the 2009 Act and discussed above. Part 4 also applies to the situation (again previously covered by the Settled Land Acts) where land is held by a minor. The only trust of land not covered by Pt 4 is a charitable trust, which is expressly excluded by s.18(9).

The identity of the trustees of land as provided for in s.19 of the 2009 Act varies depending on when the life estate/estate *pur autre vie* (described in s.19 as a strict settlement) was created. In the case of a strict settlement, the creation of which pre-dates December 1, 2009 (i.e. life estates/estates *pur autre vie* already in existence at the date of coming into effect of the 2009 Act), s.19(1)(a)(i) provides that the trustees shall be the person who would have been tenant for life within the meaning of the Settled Land Act 1882, were this statute still in operation, together with any persons who would be trustees of the settlement for the purposes of this Act. The rules for ascertaining the identity of these persons have already been discussed above.

The rules regarding trustees of life estates/estates *pur autre vie* created on or after December 1, 2009 (described by s.19(1)(a)(ii) as being the same as those applicable to express trusts created on or after that date) are laid down in s.19(1)(b) of the 2009 Act as follows:

- any trustee nominated by the trust instrument, but, if there is no such person, then,
- any person on whom the trust instrument confers a present or future power of sale of the land, or power of consent to or approval of the exercise of such a power of sale, but, if there is no such person, then,
- any person who, under either the trust instrument or the general law of trusts, has power to appoint a trustee of the land, but, if there is no such person, then,
- the settlor or, in the case of a trust created by will, the testator's personal representative or representatives.

As in the 1882 Act, there is provision for appointment of trustees by the court if necessary.

All trusts of land are stated to be governed by the general law of trusts. In addition, Pt 4 simplifies the law by stating, in s.20(1), that subject to the restrictions imposed by the trust settlement or the general law of trusts, all the powers of an owner to convey or otherwise deal with the land are conferred on the trustees. This specifically includes the power to permit a beneficiary to occupy or make other use of the land on such terms as they think fit.

The overreaching mechanism introduced by the 1882 Act is replicated in the 2009 Act in a slightly different form. Under s.21 of the 2009 Act, the sale of the property is effected by the trustees rather than the tenant for life. Payment of the purchase money to the trustees operates to transfer full title to the purchaser free of any competing equitable interests.

In the case of land held under a strict settlement or a trust of land held for persons by way of succession, or land vested in or held on trust for a minor, s.21(2)(a) provides that the conveyance must be by at least *two* trustees or a trust corporation, i.e. a corporation authorised to act as a trustee (as provided for by s.30(4) of the Succession Act 1965).

Where there is no express trust or where land is held for a minor, s.21(2)(b) provides that the conveyance may be made by a single legal owner, such as a constructive or resulting trustee. In such a case the beneficiary, or person entitled to claim an equitable interest, may protect it by registration in the Registry of Deeds (in the case of unregistered land) or Land Registry (in the case of registered land), as provided by subs.(4), the registration procedure to be prescribed by general rules under the Registration of Title Act 1964 and the Registration of Deeds and Title Act 2006.

Section 22 makes provision for resolution of disputes relating to the various trusts of land coming under Pt 4. This includes disputes between the trustees themselves, the beneficiaries themselves, the trustees and beneficiaries or the trustees or beneficiaries and other persons interested in the trust, including mortgagees or other secured creditors. The court's jurisdiction, which is summary, relates to a wide variety of matters, including the trustees' performance of their functions as trustees or other operation of the trust. It also covers disputes regarding the nature and extent of any claimed beneficial or other interest in the land.

However, s.22(3) of the 2009 Act states that, when considering an application relating to the performance by the trustees of their functions or operation of the trust, the court shall have regard to the interests of the beneficiaries as a whole and then, subject to these, to the intended purposes of the trust, the interests of any minor or person subject to any incapacity, the interests of any beneficiary's secured creditor and any other matter considered relevant by the court.

Hybrid Interests

3

Freehold ownership may be distinguished from leasehold ownership, which is the right to possession of land subject to a lease. A lease is an agreement between the freehold owner and the occupier which is intended to create a landlord and tenant relationship. The occupier under a lease is described as the leasehold owner. Leasehold ownership imposes certain obligations on the tenant, such as the duty to pay rent. It is also regulated by statute.

Normally, a landlord has a reversion; the leasehold ownership will not last forever, and when the period specified for the lease comes to an end the landlord will get his property back absolutely. However, there are some situations where a lease does last forever and these fall into the category of property interests known as hybrid interests.

Hybrid interests have both freehold and leasehold characteristics. Their freehold tendencies are evident from looking at their duration. They either last forever, akin to a fee simple, or they are determined by the length of someone's life, in a similar fashion to a life estate.

However, they have certain characteristics more appropriate to leases, in particular the fact of periodic payments to a superior owner. None of the freehold estates mentioned in the previous chapter involve the making of such payments.

These hybrid interests fall into two categories:

- leases for lives;
- fee farm grants.

I. LEASES FOR LIVES

Leases for lives are leases whose length is determined by the lives of one or more persons. Thus, the duration of such leases is determined in a manner more suitable to a freehold than a leasehold estate. However, their description as leases is not inappropriate either because they have leasehold characteristics, such as a requirement to pay rent and to observe any covenants in the lease.

The creation of leases for lives on or after December 1, 2009 has been precluded by s.14 of the Land and Conveyancing Law Reform Act 2009 (the "2009 Act") which provides that any such lease created after the coming into effect of the 2009 Act shall be void.

Existing leases for lives, however, continue in force, on the basis that these interests are so rare in modern times that what few ones exist can be left to run their course.

II. FEE FARM GRANTS

Fee farm grants involve what is essentially a fee simple estate with some leasehold characteristics, such as the holder of the fee simple being under a perpetual obligation to pay a rent to the grantor. There are three forms of fee farm grant:

- Fee farm grants which arise from subinfeudation *non obstante Quia Emptores*. As students may know from studying the medieval concept of tenure, the statute *Quia Emptores* 1290 prohibited new grants of land which created a lord/tenant relationship. After *Quia Emptores*, the only person entitled to make such grants was the King. In some cases in Ireland, the King granted tenure to certain individuals and also purported to exempt them from *Quia Emptores* and to give them permission to create new lord/tenant relationships. The result is that some property in Ireland is held under the old medieval tenure system. The holders of the land hold it as tenants under the feudal system. That is to say, they have a fee simple estate in the land but are required to pay a rent to the descendants of the grantor who are in the position of their lords. Although the tenure system is abolished by s.9 of the 2009 Act, the status of existing grants of this nature are preserved by s.9(3).

- Fee farm grants which arise under the Renewable Leasehold Conversion Act 1849 (the "1849 Act"). This Act allowed perpetually renewable leases, such as leaseholds for lives renewable forever, to be converted into fee simple. A fee farm rent is still payable to the landlord and he can forfeit for non-payment of rent or for breach of covenant. Section 74 of the Landlord and Tenant (Amendment) Act 1980 (the "1980 Act") provides that perpetually renewable leases which had not been converted under the 1849 Act were to be regarded as held in fee simple from 1980 onwards.

- Fee farm grants which arise under Deasy's Act. Deasy's Act 1860 remains one of the leading pieces of landlord and tenant legislation in Ireland. However, it blurred the distinction between leasehold and freehold ownership somewhat by providing that a reversion on the part of the landlord was not necessary for a valid lease to exist. All that was necessary was an agreement between the parties to hold as landlord and tenant, combined with the payment of rent. Thus, it is possible to have leases created under Deasy's Act which last forever.

Under the Land and Conveyancing Law Reform Act 2009, existing fee farm grants remain in force. However, s.12 of the 2009 Act prohibits the future creation of a fee farm grant by any means whatsoever by providing that any attempt, after the coming into effect of the 2009 Act, to create a fee farm grant shall simply take effect as a conveyance of a fee simple without the fee farm rent (but subject to any covenants attaching to the fee farm grant).

The section does not, however, purport to affect the validity of any fee farm grants already in existence at the date of coming into effect of the 2009 Act. The preservation of such fee farm grants is very important since a lot of property, particularly in Dublin, is held pursuant to such interests.

4 Co-Ownership

A relationship of co-ownership arises where two or more persons have a simultaneous entitlement to a particular piece of land.

I. THE FORMS OF CO-OWNERSHIP

For the purposes of most university land law courses, there are two forms of co-ownership: the joint tenancy and the tenancy in common.

JOINT TENANCY

Under a joint tenancy, each co-owner forms part of a single unit holding the land. When one joint tenant dies, a system known as survivorship applies, whereby that joint tenant's share passes to the remaining joint tenants rather than to the beneficiaries under his will or on intestacy. When all the joint tenants except one have died, the last remaining joint tenant gets the lot.

In order for co-owners to hold as joint tenants, the principles of the unit mechanism must be followed. There must be unity of time, place, interest and possession as between the joint tenants. These requirements are known as the four unities and need to be known in some detail.

Unity of possession

Each joint tenant has the right to any part of the co-owned land. One joint tenant does not have the right to fence off a particular part and exclude the other joint tenants from it.

Unity of interest

Each joint tenant must have the same estate in the land. There cannot be a joint tenancy if one co-owner has a life estate and the other has a fee simple. However, there can be a tenancy in common in such circumstances.

Unity of title

All of the co-owners' interests must have been created by the same document or transaction.

Unity of time

All of the co-owners' interests must have vested at the same time.

If the four unities are not present, there cannot be a joint tenancy, only a tenancy in common.

A joint tenancy can be terminated by one of the recognised methods for terminating co-ownership, or it can be converted into a tenancy in common by severance.

Severance of a joint tenancy at common law occurs when one or more of the four unities are lost. There are also a number of additional situations in which equity regards a joint tenancy as having been severed but the common law does not. When there is severance of a joint tenancy in equity but not at common law, the legal estate is held on a joint tenancy but the equitable estate is held on a tenancy in common.

Situations where the legal estate is held according to one form of co-ownership and the equitable estate is held on another form of co-ownership are quite common. Equity favours a tenancy in common; the common law favours a joint tenancy.

TENANCY IN COMMON

A tenancy in common is a form of co-ownership whereby each tenant in common is regarded as holding a separate share in the co-owned land. However, obviously the land has not been divided up to reflect these separate shares; if it had, there would be no co-ownership at all. The essence of a tenancy in common is that each tenant in common has a distinct, independent but undivided share in the land. Shares of tenants in common need not be equal in value. However, if a joint tenancy is severed and turned into a tenancy in common, each former joint tenant takes an equal share as tenant in common.

The four unities need not be present for a tenancy in common. Only one of them need be present, namely unity of possession. This unity is necessary for any form of co-ownership to exist.

Having distinguished between a joint tenancy and a tenancy in common, we now need to investigate the following issue which tends to feature regularly in exam problems: if two people are co-owners of property, how is it decided whether they hold under a joint tenancy or a tenancy in common?

The first step towards resolving this issue is to look at the way in which the co-ownership came into being in the first place. It is necessary to know the respective requirements for creating a joint tenancy/tenancy in common.

CO-OWNERSHIP

II. Creation of a Joint Tenancy/Tenancy in Common

Joint tenancy

For a joint tenancy to be created at common law:

(a) The four unities must be present.
(b) There must be no words of severance in the conveyance. Words of severance are words indicating that each co-owner is to take a distinct share in the property. As such, they are inconsistent with the existence of a joint tenancy. Joint tenants' shares are only assessed when the joint tenancy is turned into a tenancy in common by severance. Examples of words of severance are "equally", "in equal shares", etc.
(c) It must not fall into any of the situations recognised by equity as grounding a tenancy in common; otherwise there will be a tenancy in common of the equitable estate. These situations are as follows:
    (i) Where co-owners contribute to the purchase price in unequal shares.
    (ii) Where property is acquired by a partnership.
    (iii) Where property is conveyed to a number of people in return for a loan.
    (iv) In *Malayan Credit v Jack Chia-MPH Ltd* ([1986] A.C. 549), it was emphasised that these categories are not closed and that new situations may arise in the future where equity will be prepared to recognise a tenancy in common.

Tenancy in common

A tenancy in common of the legal estate is created when one of the four unities is absent or there are words of severance in the conveyance. If the legal estate is held on tenancy in common then the equitable estate will always be held on tenancy in common. However, even if the legal estate is held on a joint tenancy, there will still be a tenancy in common of the equitable estate if any of the four situations in (c) above are satisfied.

These are the tests which ought to be applied in deciding whether a particular form of co-ownership is created at the outset. However, that form of co-ownership may not necessarily have remained present, since a joint tenancy can be converted into a tenancy in common in a number of situations.

III. SEVERANCE OF A JOINT TENANCY

Even assuming that the form of co-ownership originally created was a joint tenancy does not settle the issue in problem questions; it may be necessary to further decide whether that joint tenancy has been *severed* at any time since its creation.

Common law traditionally treated a joint tenancy as being converted into a tenancy in common where one of the four unities was lost. If this could be proven, then a joint tenancy will be converted into a tenancy in common both at law and in equity. For example, if one of the joint tenants acquires a greater estate in the land, then there will be no unity of interest. Alternatively, if one of the joint tenants conveyed his interest to a third party who was not a co-owner, there will be no unity of title.

This applied even if the conveyance were effected by operation of law. In the case of *Containercare (Ireland) Ltd v Wycherley* ([1982] I.R. 143) the court granted a judgment mortgage over co-owned property. It was held that this had the effect of severing the joint tenancy.

In addition, equity treated a joint tenancy as being severed in three additional situations, laid down in *Williams v Hensman* ((1861) 1 J. & H. 546) and affirmed in *Byrne v Byrne* (unreported, High Court, January 18, 1980):

- Where a joint tenant enters into a contract to transfer his land to someone else.
- Where there is a mutual agreement between the joint tenants to sever.
- Where joint tenants behave in a manner which indicates that they now regard themselves as holding under a tenancy in common.

The law in relation to severance of a joint tenancy was substantially amended by s.30 of the Land and Conveyancing Law Reform Act 2009 (the "2009 Act") which abolished, with effect from December 1, 2009, unilateral severance by a single joint tenant without the written consent of all the other joint tenant(s). The consequence is that it is no longer possible for a joint tenant to sever a joint tenancy by selling his interest or acquiring an additional interest or entering into a contract to do same unless he has obtained the consent of the other joint tenants to such severance or has obtained a court order dispensing with such consent (a court has jurisdiction under s.31 to make such an order where consent to severance is being unreasonably withheld).

Section 30 also makes it clear that from December 1, 2009 the registration of a judgment mortgage against one of the owners of property held under a joint tenancy no longer operates to effect a severance of that joint tenancy.

CO-OWNERSHIP

The joint tenancy remains unsevered despite the registration of the judgment mortgage, and is extinguished on the death of the judgment debtor.

Section 30 limits unilateral severance only and does not in any way prejudice the right of a joint tenant to claim severance in equity by mutual agreement or course of dealing.

IV. DETERMINATION OF CO-OWNERSHIP

There are a number of ways in which a situation of co-ownership may come to an end.

UNION IN A SOLE TENANT

This occurs either through survivorship or through one tenant buying out the other.

PARTITION

Previously, partition (the physical division of the property) could be ordered by the court under the Partition Acts 1868–1876 where agreement could not be reached between the co-owners. Section 31 of the 2009 Act repeals the Partition Acts 1868–1876 and replaces them with a a new statutory jurisdiction to make a wide range of orders at the behest of any person (including a secured creditor or trustee) having an estate or interest in co-owned land. Such orders are not confined to directing partition or sale and division of the proceeds and include directing accounting adjustments as between the co-owners.

SALE

As discussed above in relation to partition, sale can be effected by agreement of the co-owners or alternatively by order of the court under s.31 of the 2009 Act.

Easements

5

An easement may be defined as a proprietary right which accrues to an individual by virtue of his ownership of land and which enables him to perform some act on the land of a neighbouring landowner which would otherwise constitute a trespass.

In total, four characteristics are necessary for an easement to exist. First, because an easement is annexed to land, the person asserting the right must be able to show that he owns land in the neighbourhood of the land over which the right is exercised and that his land is benefited by the exercise of the right. In other words:

1. There must be a dominant and a servient tenement.
2. The dominant and servient tenements must not be owned and occupied by the same person.
3. The easement must benefit the dominant tenement.
4. The right must be capable of forming the subject-matter of a grant. This has been summarised as meaning that it must be precisely defined and similar in nature to those rights historically established as easements.

I. CHARACTERISTICS OF AN EASEMENT

THERE MUST BE A DOMINANT AND A SERVIENT TENEMENT

As stated above, this follows logically from the fact that an easement is an incorporeal hereditament annexed to land.

For example, Alfred claims a right of way over Edith's land. Alfred must show that he has land in the vicinity of Edith's land which is benefited by the exercise of this right of way. Alfred's land is the dominant tenement; it gets the benefit of the alleged easement. Edith's land is the servient tenement; it bears the burden of the easement.

THE DOMINANT AND SERVIENT TENEMENTS MUST NOT BE OWNED AND OCCUPIED BY THE SAME PERSON

The word "and" in the above sentence is very important. It is not necessarily a bar to the recognition of an easement that the dominant and servient tenements are held in common ownership, provided that they are occupied by

EASEMENTS

different persons. For example, a tenant may acquire an easement against his landlord or against another tenant. This has been established in Ireland since the case of *Hanna v Pollock* ([1900] 2 I.R. 664).

THE EASEMENT MUST ACCOMMODATE THE DOMINANT TENEMENT

The easement must benefit the dominant tenement in some way. This means that it must benefit the owner in his capacity as landowner, rather than in a personal capacity. It must enhance his enjoyment of the dominant tenement.

In *Hill v Tupper* ((1863) 2 H. & C. 121) the lessee of land adjoining a canal was granted the exclusive right by his neighbour, who owned the canal, to hire out pleasure boats on it. The issue was whether this right amounted to an easement or a licence. The court said that it was not an easement because the exclusive right to hire out pleasure boats on the canal was a commercial monopoly and, although it benefited the neighbouring owner as a business-man, it did not actually benefit him in the use of his riverbank land.

The merits of this decision have been much debated. At times it is difficult to draw the line between benefiting an individual in his use of land and benefiting him personally. It is important to remember that the courts are reluctant to recognise new easements which appear to fall harshly on the owner of the servient tenement. The right in this case was an exclusive one, and of a commercial nature. Recognising it would effectively deprive the owner of the servient tenement of the right to one of the potential sources of income from his property, i.e. the canal pleasure boat trade.

A contrasting case is that of *Moody v Steggles* ((1879) 12 Ch D 261). Here it was held that the right of the owner of a public house to place a sign on adjoining premises advertising his business was capable of being an easement. The judge in this case felt that the right to advertise one's business on a neighbouring land was capable of enhancing one's use of the land.

Therefore, it should not be understood that a right which enhances a business carried on by the owner of the dominant tenement on his land is automatically incapable of qualifying as an easement. Instead, it is worth using these cases to make the point that there is no clear-cut rule in relation to new kinds of rights, as to whether they are capable of qualifying as easements or not.

What can be said is that the court will have considerations of justice in mind in answering this question and is unlikely to recognise rights as easements if they bear heavily on the owner of the servient tenement. Where the recognition of certain rights would lead to this problem, the courts will usually manage to exclude them by saying either that they do not benefit the dominant tenement or by saying that they are incapable of forming the subject-matter of a grant. Usually the latter mechanism is utilised, but in *Hill v Tupper* it was the former one which was employed.

THE RIGHT MUST BE CAPABLE OF FORMING THE SUBJECT-MATTER OF A GRANT

This requirement has two sub-components.

(a) The scope of the right must be precise and clear

The courts will not impose vague restrictions on the right to possession of the owner of the servient tenement. An example would be the reluctance to recognise a general right to a view, which was displayed in *Dalton v Angus & Co* ((1881) 6 App. Cas. 740). A widely recognised right to a view would seriously restrict building and, in addition to being questionable from the public policy point of view, would disproportionately restrict the development potential of the servient tenement.

(b) The right must be similar in nature to those rights historically recognised as easements

There are certain long-established easements: the right to light; rights of way; and the right to support from an adjoining building. In *Dyce v Hay* ((1852) 1 Macq. 305 at 312–313) Lord St. Leonards stated:

> "The category of servitudes and easements must alter and expand with the changes that take place in the circumstances of mankind."

Nonetheless, the courts subject new easements to careful scrutiny.

Copeland v Greenhalf ([1952] Ch. 488) involved a wheelwright who was allowed by his neighbour to use part of his yard for repairing vehicles and to store some of the vehicles there. He argued that this right was an easement. This was rejected as the claimant was practically alleging a right to possession of part of his neighbour's property.

In the contrasting case of *Wright v Macadam* ([1949] 2 K.B. 744), it was held that the right to exclusive use of a coal shed could constitute an easement. In *Middleton v Clarence* ((1877) 11 I.R.C.L. 499), the right to throw spoil on a neighbour's land amounted to an easement.

The difficulty with recognising rights of storage and parking as capable of being easements is that this necessarily leads to an overlap between the rules on easements and the doctrine of adverse possession. Should an individual who stores property in a neighbour's shed be able to claim either a de facto title to the shed by adverse possession or, alternatively, an easement of storage, depending on which set of criteria suit him best?

This overlap is a very real possibility given that *Griffin v Bleithin* ([1999] 2 I.L.R.M. 182) regarded the defendant's behaviour in storing property in a shed as demonstrating sufficient *animus possidendi* to extinguish the title of the original owner of the shed (see Chapter 11 for further detail on this case).

In *Phipps v Pears* ([1965] 1 Q.B. 76), it was held that there was no easement which guaranteed a building shelter from the wind and rain. In contrast with this case is the judgment of the Supreme Court in *Treacy v Dublin Corporation* ([1993] 1 I.R. 305), the leading Irish case on the characteristics of an easement. In this case, a right of protection from the weather was held to be necessary in order to ensure that an easement of support was observed. However, the right was dependent on the particular facts of the case and did not differ from *Phipps v Pears* in this regard.

The ancillary rights doctrine put forward in *Treacy* is a method whereby rights not otherwise qualifying as easements can be raised to the status of easements by treating them as necessary for the enjoyment of other rights which exist and which are definitely categorised as easements. For example, it has yet to be conclusively decided in Ireland whether the right to park constitutes an easement or not. It has been argued that such a right should be recognised as an easement, at least where it is necessary for the enjoyment of established easements such as rights of way. In *Redfont Ltd v Custom House Dock Management Ltd* (unreported, High Court, Shanley J., March 31, 1998), it was held on an interlocutory application that the plaintiffs had raised a fair issue to be tried as to whether an ancillary right to park cars was reasonably necessary to substantially enjoy certain rights of way granted to them as sub-tenants in the Irish Financial Services Centre.

The test that the courts are applying in this category has been described as an examination of whether the right is analogous to those historically listed as easements. As with the previous requirement that the easement benefit the dominant tenement, this test initially appears clear-cut, but on closer examination may be a difficult question to decide. This is not helped by the fact that much of the case law cited above appears contradictory.

However, the cases are not as contradictory as they appear. In deciding whether to recognise new forms of easement, most of the judgments are taking similar factors into account.

The key determining factors are as follows:

- The hardship that the recognition of such an easement is likely to cause to owners of servient tenements. A major sub-factor here is whether the alleged right compels the owner of the servient tenement to incur expenditure or perform positive duties.
- Public policy considerations, including the long-term consequences of the decision.
- Whether such a right is more appropriately achieved by use of other legal mechanisms such as restrictive covenants or licences.

II. ACQUISITION OF EASEMENTS

If an easement is being claimed over someone else's property, it is not enough to show that the right asserted satisfies the characteristics of an easement as set out at Section I above. It must also be shown that the claimant acquired this right in some recognised way.

There are three main ways in which easements may be acquired:

- By express grant or reservation.
- By implied grant or reservation.
- By prescription.

As a preliminary point, it is necessary to outline the difference between a grant of an easement and a reservation of an easement. A reservation occurs where the vendor/lessor of land reserves an easement over the land sold/leased for the benefit of neighbouring land retained by him. A grant, on the other hand, usually occurs where the purchaser/lessee of land, in addition to getting the land he has purchased/leased, also gets easements over adjoining land which has been retained by the vendor/lessor. A grant of an easement (but not a reservation) may also occur independently of a sale of the dominant tenement.

ACQUISITION BY EXPRESS GRANT/RESERVATION

This occurs when the grant or reservation is expressly stated in a document. The document may either be a document selling or leasing the dominant tenement or it may be an independent document designed specifically to transfer the easement in isolation.

ACQUISITION BY IMPLIED GRANT/RESERVATION

Implied easements are easements which are not granted expressly by the owner of the servient tenement but which are implied by the courts in situations where an individual sells or leases part of his land. Implied easements may either be implied grants, i.e. for the benefit of the part sold, or implied reservations, i.e. for the benefit of the part retained.

Implied reservations

The courts do not like the idea of easements arising by reservation. Just as they construe express reservations strictly, so they are reluctant to imply reservations in a sale/lease for the benefit of the vendor/lessor. Until recently, the situations in which implied reservations could arise were thought to be very limited.

Traditionally, there were only two situations in which the courts were prepared to imply easements in a conveyance for the benefit of the vendor/lessor. The first was in the case of landlocked land: where the vendor/lessor had sold/leased all the land around the part retained and would have no legally enforceable way of entering or leaving his property if he were not granted a right of way over the part sold/leased. The courts have characterised this as an **easement of necessity:** it would be impossible for the owner of the dominant tenement to have any use of his property were the easement not granted.

The second situation arose in relation to the easement of support. Where an individual owns two houses with a common supporting wall and sells one of them, he is regarded as retaining an easement of support in relation to the house sold. In other words, the purchaser cannot demolish the house he has bought if to do so would mean the collapse of the vendor's house. This is explained as an **easement of common intention:** in situations where one of two adjoining houses is sold and the other is retained by the vendor, it must be taken to be the intention of both parties to the conveyance that the purchaser should not demolish the house he has bought if to do so would cause the vendor's house to fall down.

However, the recent judgment of Kinlen J. in *Dwyer Nolan Developments Ltd v Kingscroft Developments Ltd* ([1999] 1 I.L.R.M. 141) is indicative of an Irish trend towards expanding the circumstances in which reservations may be implied.

In *Dwyer Nolan*, the plaintiff, a property developer, sold some of his land to the defendant, another property developer. This sale effectively left the land retained by the plaintiff landlocked, but at the time of the transfer the defendant had a grant of planning permission which provided for an access road from the plaintiff's property to the main road. The plaintiff intended to develop the retained land and the defendant knew of this intention.

However, subsequent to the transfer, the defendant got an alteration of the planning permission which abolished the access road from the plaintiff's property to the main road. The plaintiff still had some access in and out of his lands under the new planning permission, but by foot rather than by road. This made it impossible for the plaintiff to develop the land; however, it was still possible for him to use it for agricultural purposes.

United Kingdom authority on the subject indicated that when a right of way of necessity arose in relation to landlocked land retained by a vendor, that right of way was limited to such access rights as were necessary for the purposes for which the land was being used at the time of the transfer. Although the plaintiff was entitled to a right of way, he was only entitled to a right of way for agricultural use, because that was the only use to which the land was being put at the time of the transfer.

However, Kinlen J. preferred to follow Irish authority to the contrary and, in so doing, adopted a much more relaxed attitude to the doctrine of easements of necessity. He stated that the retained land had always been understood by both parties to be development land intended for industrial use. The plaintiff was entitled to such right of way as was necessary for this use.

It is interesting to compare the judgment of Kinlen J. in *Dwyer Nolan* with the even more recent decision of the Court of Appeal in *Peckham v Ellison* ([1999] Conv. 353). A local council sold off a council house to the defendant and retained a neighbouring house. They subsequently sold the neighbouring house to the plaintiff. The plaintiff claimed that a reservation in favour of the council was implied in the conveyance to the plaintiff. This easement would then have passed to the plaintiff when the council subsequently sold him the dominant tenement. The reservation alleged was a right of way for all purposes around the side and across the rear of the plaintiff's house.

It was held that the right of way in question had been reserved by implication in the conveyance to the defendant. It was necessary to imply this right to give effect to the common intention of the parties. Had the council and the defendant thought about it when the house was being sold, this easement would have been expressly reserved in favour of the council.

It may be seen that there is a growing trend on the part of both the United Kingdom and Irish courts to imply reservations into a conveyance. The correctness of such an approach is questionable and conflicts with traditional authority on easements. The broad approach taken to the concepts of necessity and common intention in the above cases may also result in an increase in the number of implied grants.

Implied grants

All implied grants are theoretically based on the intention of the parties to the land transfer. Therefore they may be rebutted by evidence of an express contrary intention in the document effecting the transfer. In addition, the rules regarding implied grants of easements only come into operation if the land transfer is a voluntary one. No easements will be implied in a conveyance or lease which is involuntary, for example one required by statute.

As with reservations, grants may be implied on the basis of necessity or common intention.

Prior to the coming into effect of the Land and Conveyancing Law Reform Act 2009 (the "2009 Act"), easements by implied grant could also be acquired under the rule in *Wheeldon v Burrows* ((1879) 12 Ch D 31), which implied into a conveyance or lease of the dominant tenement all quasi-easements exercised over the servient tenement prior to the conveyance or lease, provided that they were necessary for the reasonable enjoyment of the land granted, and continuous and apparent.

Section 40 of the 2009 Act replaces *Wheeldon v Burrows* with a simpler rule, allowing the implication of easements in favour of a purchaser where they are: (a) necessary for the reasonable enjoyment of the part disposed of, and (b) it was reasonable for the parties, or would have been had they adverted to the matter, to assume that the easements were implied in the disposition. Section 40 does not, however, affect implied easements of necessity or common intention or easements implied pursuant to the doctrine of non-derogation from grant, which continue to apply in full.

Another way in which easements were implied prior to the coming into effect of the 2009 Act was pursuant to s.6 of the Conveyancing Act 1881, which operated to imply easements into a conveyance (as defined by the Act) where there had been different persons in occupation of the dominant and servient tenements prior to the conveyance and the easement in question had been enjoyed as a quasi-easement by the occupier of the dominant tenement over the servient tenement prior to and up to the time of the conveyance.

Section 6 has also been repealed by the 2009 Act and accordingly this ground for implying easements no longer applies in relation to conveyances which post-date the 2009 Act (although as with *Wheeldon v Burrows*, it presumably can still be relied on to make an argument for implied easements arising out of conveyances which pre-date the 2009 Act).

It should be noted that, as with *Wheeldon v Burrows* and s.6, s.40 of the 2009 Act only applies to implied grants and not to implied reservations.

ACQUISITION BY PRESCRIPTION

Express and implied easements have this in common: there must be some kind of land transfer from the owner of the servient tenement to the owner of the dominant tenement in order for them to exist. However, easements which arise by prescription are easements which are acquired by long user.

Prescription under the pre-2009 Act regime

Under the law applicable prior to the coming into effect of the 2009 Act (which law continues to be capable of being relied on in proceedings initiated prior to December 1, 2021) there were two main conditions which had to be fulfilled in order to acquire easements by prescription. First, that the claimant or his predecessors in title must have been in the habit of using the easement as if it belonged to them. Secondly, that user of this kind has to have gone on for a specific period of time preceding the date of the court action.

As regards the type of user required, the prima facie rule was that the user must have been without force, without secrecy and without permission. Permissive user merely created a licence, not an easement by prescription. However, the Prescription Act 1832 (as applied in Ireland by the Prescription (Ireland) Act 1858) modified the ban on permissive user to some extent by holding that permissive user might give rise to an easement by prescription if it had gone on for an extra-long period of time (40 years instead of the 20 years normally required for non-permissive user) and the user had not been enjoyed by written permission. An easement of light was acquired after only 20 years provided once again that it had not been enjoyed with written permission.

As regards easements other than light, s.1 of the Act provided for acquisition of these easements after 20 years' user as of right continuing up to the time of the court action. As stated above, easements exercised with oral (but not written) permission could be acquired under the Act after 40 years' user.

The Act was supplemented by the common law doctrine of lost modern grant, which allowed the acquisition of easements after 20 years' user as of right but did not require the 20-year period to be continuous up to the date of the court action in which the prescriptive rights were being claimed.

PRESCRIPTION UNDER THE 2009 ACT REGIME

The Land and Conveyancing Law Reform Act 2009 lays down a new regime in relation to prescription. The main changes here relate to the acquisition of easements and profits by prescription. The old methods of prescription detailed above are replaced by a single method detailed in ss.34 to 37, whereby 12 years' user as of right and without interruption gives rise to an easement or profit by prescription. However, in order to protect State authorities which own tracts of land, including the foreshore, every part of which it is impracticable to keep under constant supervision, extended periods of user of 30 years (non-foreshore) and 60 years (foreshore) are required in the case of land owned by the State. In addition, where the owner of the servient tenement is subject to a mental incapacity, this interrupts the prescriptive period, up to a maximum of 30 years (s.37).

Section 35, as amended by s.57 of the Civil Law (Miscellaneous Provisions) Act 2011, further provides that title to an easement or profit will not be obtained "at law" unless and until the claimant obtains a court order to this effect and such order is registered in the Registry of Deeds (if the claim relates to unregistered land) or Land Registry (if it relates to registered land) or unless registration of same is permitted by the Land Registry without a court order.

The relevant user period upon which such claim is based should be that immediately before the commencement of the claimant's action (s.35(2)) with a discretion of the court to allow acquisition by prescription, even where the user period was not immediately before commencement, where it is just and equitable to do so in the circumstances of the case (s.35(3)).

Section 36 deals with the position where the prescriptive claim relates to land subject to a tenancy. Subsection 36(1) provides that where the claimant by prescription holds a tenancy only in the land which the easement or profit à prendre benefits, the easement or profit attaches to the land and, when the tenancy ends, it passes with the land to the landlord. Conversely, where the easement or profit is exercisable over land which is currently occupied by a tenant, it ends with the tenancy unless the tenant either acquires a superior interest (in which case it attaches to it) or an extension or renewal of the tenancy (in which case it attaches to that extension or renewal).

Section 38, as amended by s.38 of the Civil Law (Miscellaneous Provisions) Act 2011, provides that where the period of user required under the existing law was actually or was close to being completed before the commencement, but the court action to claim the easement or profit is not made until after that commencement of the 2009 Act, the claimant can rely on the old law provided the action is brought within 12 years of that commencement. This effectively allows a prescriptive claimant to rely on the old law detailed above in any proceedings issued before December 1, 2021. However, once this transitional period has expired, any subsequent claim must rely upon the new provisions in Chapter 1.

Section 39 modifies the law relating to extinguishment of easements and profits by raising a presumption that a 12-year continuous period of non-user will operate to extinguish easements and profits à prendre acquired by prescription or by implication. This presumption will not apply where the easement or profit has been protected by registration in the Registry of Deeds or Land Registry. Significantly, s.39 allows a period prior to the coming into effect of the 2009 Act to count for the purpose of the 12 years, provided that at least three years of the period of non-user occur after the commencement of the 2009 Act.

Freehold Covenants

6

Sometimes the owner of land enters into a deed with his neighbour in which he promises to refrain from carrying out some act on his land or, more rarely, to perform some act in relation to it. This often occurs when an individual purchases land and the vendor wants to protect adjoining land which he is retaining. The vendor requires the purchaser to enter into a freehold covenant with him as a condition of the sale. These covenants are known as freehold covenants, to distinguish them from covenants contained in leases. They represent a restriction on the freehold owner's right to freely use his land.

The person who has the right to sue on the covenant is known as the covenantee and the person who is bound by the restriction and liable to be sued if he breaches it is known as the covenantor.

Issues in relation to freehold covenants are twofold. It is clear that they bind the covenantor vis-à-vis the covenantee. Such is self-evident under ordinary principles of contract law. What is less clear is the extent to which they run with the land to bind successors in title of the covenantor and/or to empower successors in title of the covenantee to invoke them in court.

Thus, two principal questions arise regarding covenants entered into in relation to freehold land:

- First, assuming the original covenantee to have parted with his land, to what extent does the benefit of the covenant run with the land of the covenantee to allow it to be invoked by his successors in title?

- Secondly, assuming the original covenantor to have parted with his land, does the burden of the covenant run with the land of the covenantor so as to bind his successors in title?

It is traditional in land law exams to set problem questions on the topic of freehold covenants. There are four scenarios upon which the student may be required to advise. Take the following example:

A sells part of his land to B. As a condition of the transfer, B covenants not to put up any new buildings on the land he has purchased.

- Can A sue B if B breaches this covenant?
- If A sells his land on to C, can C invoke the covenant to stop B building on his land?

- Conversely, if A retains his land while B sells on his land to D, can A enforce the covenant against D?
- What if both A and B have parted with their land? Can A's successor in title, C, enforce the covenant against B's successor in title, D?

The first example, which involves the enforcement of the covenant by the original covenantee against the original covenantor, can be dealt with in contract without having to rely on land law rules at all. Since A and B are the original parties to the covenant, A should have no difficulty in enforcing it against B.

As regards the other three scenarios outlined, we need to distinguish between freehold covenants, the creation of which pre-dates the coming into effect of the Land and Conveyancing Law Reform Act 2009 (the "2009 Act") on December 1, 2009 and those created on or after that date.

I. ENFORCEMENT OF POST-DECEMBER 2009 FREEHOLD COVENANTS

As regards covenants in respect of land, the creation of which post-dates December 1, 2009, the situation is relatively simple—the law on their enforceability is now set out in s.49 of the 2009 Act, which provides that the benefit of such a covenant, whether positive or negative, will run with the land intended to be benefited and the burden will run with the land subject to the covenant. The benefit and burden will attach to the owners for the time being of the lands in question. A person who has ceased to be the owner of the benefited land may enforce breaches of covenant which occurred before he or she ceased to be the owner, and a person who has ceased to be the owner of the benefited land may also also be liable for breaches which occurred during their period of ownership.

It is, however, possible to contract out of the new provisions, by making it clear that a particular covenant is personal to a party or parties and does not pass to their successors in title (s.49(6)(b) which states that s.49 takes effect subject to the terms of the covenant or the instrument containing it).

II. ENFORCEMENT OF PRE-DECEMBER 2009 FREEHOLD COVENANTS

Matters are more complicated in respect of covenants which pre-date the 2009 Act. In this case, the statutory provisions do not apply and the law is as set out by the common law and equity.

We need to distinguish between three different situations:

(i) Enforcement against the original covenantor by a successor in title of the covenantee;
(ii) Enforcement against a successor in title of the covenantor by the original covenantee;
(iii) Enforcement against a successor in title of the covenantor by a successor in title of the covenantee.

i) ENFORCEMENT AGAINST THE ORIGINAL COVENANTOR BY A SUCCESSOR IN TITLE OF THE COVENANTEE

In order for this to occur:

(a) The covenant must touch and concern the land of the covenantee. This means that the covenant must not be of personal benefit to the covenantee only. It must benefit him in his capacity as landowner.
(b) The successor in title to the original covenantee must own a legal estate in the land. The reason for this is that the common law does not normally recognise equitable interests in land, and will not allow the common law rules to be used to recognise benefits which are attached to an equitable estate.
(c) The successor in title to the original covenantee must possess the same type of estate as the original covenantee. The consequence of this is that a tenant cannot enforce a freehold covenant entered into by his landlord. Also, a tenant in tail or the holder of a life estate cannot enforce a covenant entered into for the benefit of a fee simple predecessor in title.

If a successor in title of the covenantee cannot bring himself within the common law rules for passing of the benefit, he may nevertheless be able to make a case for passing of the benefit in equity. The equitable requirements for passing of benefit are detailed later in this chapter.

ii) ENFORCEMENT AGAINST A SUCCESSOR IN TITLE OF THE COVENANTOR BY THE ORIGINAL COVENANTEE

The common law position is that the burden of a freehold covenant cannot be tied to the land of the covenantor and will not be allowed to bind future owners of that land.

However, the area of freehold covenants is one of the situations in which equity has intervened to modify the common law.

Under the rule in *Tulk v Moxhay* ((1848) 2 Ph. 774), the burden of a freehold covenant may run with the land in equity so that future owners of the covenantor's land are bound by it. This diverges from the common law view.

The facts of Tulk v Moxhay

The facts of *Tulk v Moxhay* were as follows: the plaintiff, Mr Tulk, sold a garden to E, requiring E to enter into a covenant to the effect that the land would be kept as a garden and not be covered by any buildings. E sold the land, and it passed through the hands of a number of people until it was purchased by the defendant, Mr Moxhay, who purchased it with notice of the covenant. Although Mr Moxhay knew of the covenant, he tried to build on the land. Mr Tulk brought an action to stop him on the ground that he was in breach of covenant. Mr Moxhay argued that he was not bound by the covenant. He cited the common law rule that the burden does not pass to successors in title of the covenantor.

It was held that an injunction could be granted in equity against Mr Moxhay restraining him from breaching the restrictive covenant. The burden of a restrictive covenant ran with the land in equity. Conditions (a)–(d) above were satisfied. The covenant was a restrictive one and Mr Moxhay had had notice of it. In addition, Mr Tulk, the original covenantee, had retained land in the vicinity of the square which was benefited by the covenant. As a continuing householder in the area, it was in his interest to see that the land was not built up.

Under the rule in *Tulk v Moxhay* equity will regard successors in title of the covenantor as bound by the terms of the covenant if the following conditions are satisfied:

(a) The covenant must be a negative or restrictive covenant. It must not impose positive obligations on the covenantor, but rather, must restrict him from doing something.

In *Rhone v Stephens* ([1994] 2 A.C. 310), the roof of a house partly covered an adjoining property. The owner of the house had a covenant with his adjoining neighbour that he would keep the common roof tiled and water tight. The covenantor's property came into new hands. Could the covenant be enforced against the new owners? The House of Lords refused to enforce this covenant against the covenantor's successor in title because it was a covenant which carried positive obligations; the rule in *Tulk v Moxhay* only applied to restrictive covenants.

In deciding whether a covenant is positive or negative the courts will look behind the language in which the covenant is framed to the substance of the obligation in question. For example, in *Tulk v Moxhay*, the covenant in question was expressed in positive language as involving a duty to maintain the square as a garden.

However, when one looked behind the wording to the substance of the obligation involved it became apparent that what was actually involved was a restrictive covenant prohibiting building.

(b) The land to which the benefit of the covenant is attached must be in the vicinity of the burdened land and must be benefited by the covenant.

(c) The right to sue a successor in title of the covenantor is an equitable proprietary interest. As such, we must decide whether the new owner should be bound by applying the general rules for deciding whether third party interests bind the transferee of land. These rules differ depending on whether the covenantor's land is registered or unregistered.

The burden imposed by *Tulk v Moxhay* is an equitable burden. As such, if existing over unregistered land, it can be extinguished by a sale of the legal estate in the land to a bona fide purchaser for value who has no actual or constructive notice of the covenant. Therefore, if the successor in title can show that he is the owner of the legal estate, that he gave consideration for the transfer, and that he had no actual, constructive or imputed notice of the covenant, he will not be bound by it.

If the land burdened by the covenant is registered, then a purchaser of that land will not be bound unless the covenant is marked on the Register as a burden. However, if the successor in title of the covenantor has received the land as a gift, then he will be bound by the covenant whether it is marked on the Register or not.

(d) The rule in *Tulk v Moxhay* may only be invoked by the original covenantee if he retains the land for the benefit of which the covenant was entered into.

There is one other requirement which we do not have to worry about in this situation as A is the original covenantee:

(e) The rule in *Tulk v Moxhay* may only be invoked by successors in title of the original covenantee if they can show that the benefit of the covenant has passed to them in equity. Showing passing of benefit at common law is not enough to justify appealing to the equitable rules on passing of burden and vice versa. This requirement will be discussed in the next section of the chapter.

iii) Enforcement against a successor in title of the covenantor by a successor in title of the covenantee

As we have seen, a successor in title of the original covenantor may be sued under *Tulk v Moxhay* in equity, but all the necessary constituents of this rule must be satisfied. In particular, condition (e) in *Tulk v Moxhay*, which was briefly mentioned above, assumes great importance in this scenario.

Condition (e) states that, if the person trying to invoke *Tulk v Moxhay* is not the original covenantee but a successor in title, then he must show that the benefit of the covenant has passed to him in equity. This can be quite a difficult condition to fulfil as the benefit does not pass as easily in equity as at common law.

The benefit of the covenant will only pass in equity if:

(a) the covenant touches and concerns the land of the covenantee;
(b) the land owned by the covenantee is now owned by the applicant; and
(c) one of the following three conditions is satisfied:
    (i) The benefit of the covenant was annexed to the land.
    (ii) The benefit of the covenant was assigned with the land.
    (iii) The land benefited and the land burdened were part of a scheme of development.

The first two conditions are straightforward. However, there is a lot of case law on the various components of condition (c). Remember that only one of these components need be fulfilled in order for the benefit to pass in equity. We will now go on to look at each of the components in turn.

Annexation

This requires that at the time the covenant was created, both parties to the covenant intended that the benefit of the covenant should run with the land, i.e. that the covenant could be invoked by successors in title of the covenantee. This intention is evident where the covenant states that it is made for the benefit of the land or that it is made with the covenantee in his capacity as landowner. Both statements are regarded as demonstrating an intention that future owners of the land should have the benefit of the covenant.

For example, in *Rogers v Hosegood* ([1900] 2 Ch. 388), a restrictive covenant was held to be annexed to the land of the covenantee because it was stated to be in favour of the vendors of certain land, their assigns and others claiming under them, for the benefit of adjoining land. The scope of the property to which the covenant is to be annexed must be clearly defined. This was not the case in *Renals v Cowlishaw* ((1878) 9 Ch D 125), where a claim of annexation failed for this reason.

In addition, the property described as property to which the covenant is annexed should be property which is touched and concerned by the covenant, otherwise the annexation may be struck down as too wide. In *Re Ballard's Conveyance* ([1937] Ch. 473), the benefit of the covenant was annexed to an estate of 1700 acres. Only a small part of this land was capable of being benefited by the covenant. It was held that the covenant was not enforceable by the purchasers of the estate.

One unresolved issue relates to the possibility of statutory annexation of all covenants of freehold land so that their benefit automatically runs with the land in equity. Section 58 of the Conveyancing Act 1881 provides as follows: "A freehold covenant shall be deemed to be made with the covenantee and his heirs and assigns". It has been argued that this provision has the effect of annexing all freehold covenants to the covenantee's land in equity so that the benefit of them automatically runs with the land. However, the balance of academic authority is against the statutory annexation argument.

Assignment

When the covenant is not annexed to the land so as to run automatically with it, there is still a possibility that the benefit may run with the land if it is passed on expressly in every assignment of that land. The assignment of the covenant must be contemporaneous with the assignment of the land. Hence, once the land has been sold the covenant cannot be subsequently assigned.

However, what happens if the covenant benefits a particular area of land and part of the land from that area is sold off without the benefit being transferred? Given that the land retained is still benefited by the covenant, can the covenant be later transferred to the purchaser? *Re Union of London and Smith's Bank Ltd's Conveyance* ([1933] Ch. 611) answers this question in the negative.

Scheme of development

This is a peculiar doctrine of equity used to control housing estates and developments. The objective of many estate planners is that each house in the estate should be subject to similar restrictive covenants, in order to ensure the correct appearance and maintenance of the estate. The aim of the estate planners is that each house in the estate should be bound by these covenants and that the householder should also be able to enforce them against other owners of houses in the estate. In such a situation, equity will recognise a passing of the burden without looking for annexation or assignment.

The original way of achieving mutual benefit and burden consisted of arranging for the sale of all the houses on the estate to be sold at the one time and for the purchasers to enter into a deed of mutual covenant at the time of sale. However, in most cases, houses on an estate would not all be sold at the same time.

Therefore, equity developed a more pragmatic solution. Equity provides that the purchaser of a house in a scheme of development only needs to covenant with the vendor. Even though there is no actual agreement with owners of houses which have been previously sold, equity regards these as being within the benefit of the covenant. Everyone living within the scheme of development can enforce these covenants against anyone else living within the scheme.

A scheme of development occurs where there is a development within a clearly defined area, with all property holders within the area intended to be subject to a framework of mutual rights and obligations. The purchasers of property within the development must be aware of the scope of the development, and the particular rights and obligations attached to it. It is difficult to explain the rationale behind this doctrine, and it has been remarked that it may be one of those branches of equity which works best when explained least.

In order for the reciprocal obligations and rights to apply, the following conditions must be fulfilled:

1. The same vendor must have owned all the land subject to the scheme originally.
2. Before selling the land, the vendor must have divided the land into lots subject to common restrictions.

    This requirement is not applied strictly, as is shown by the case of *Baxter v Four Oaks Properties Ltd* ([1965] Ch. 816) and *Re Dolphin's Conveyance* ([1970] Ch. 654).
3. The restrictions must be of benefit to all the lots.
4. There must be disclosure of the nature and terms of the scheme to individual purchasers. They must know that the rights and obligations are reciprocal and they must know their content.
5. The area within which the scheme operates must be definite and known to the participants. Otherwise they will not be aware of the scope of their rights and obligations.

To summarise the law on this issue, a successor in title of the covenantee may sue a successor in title of the covenantor under *Tulk v Moxhay*, provided that he can satisfy the first four conditions in *Tulk v Moxhay* and also show that the benefit has passed to him in equity either by annexation, assignment or under the scheme of development principle.

III. EXTINGUISHMENT OF FREEHOLD COVENANTS

Section 50 of the Land and Conveyancing Law Reform Act 2009 contains new provisions entitling a person subject to a freehold covenant to apply for a court order discharging it in whole or in part, or modifying it on the ground that it now constitutes an unreasonable interference with the use and enjoyment of the land subject to it. Unlike s.49, s.50 applies to covenants which pre-date as well as post-date the coming into effect of the 2009 Act.

Section 50(2) sets out various matters to which the court must have regard in determining whether to make an order, including: changes in the character of the lands affected by the covenant; what benefit, if any, it still secures; and whether continued compliance has become unduly onerous compared with that benefit. The court may include as part of its order a requirement that compensation is paid to cover a quantifiable loss resulting from the order.

7

Licences and Estoppel

The distinction between personal and proprietary rights has been fundamental to the law on licences. A proprietary right is an interest over land which binds third parties. It may be sold or transferred by will. Some proprietary rights such as easements and the right to sue under restrictive covenants are annexed to land which is benefited by them and cannot be sold independently of the land. However, they can be transferred with the land.

A personal right, on the other hand, only exists as between two specific individuals. It is personal to those individuals. The person who has the right cannot transfer it to anyone else, and the right cannot bind third parties who purchase the land over which it has been granted.

A licence is a permission to occupy or exercise a right over land which is owned by somebody else. The person who is granted the right is known as the licensee. The owner of the land, the person who grants him the right is known as the licensor. A licence is generally understood to be a personal right. However, one development which casts a shadow on that assumption has been the appearance of a new category of licence known as the estoppel licence.

The equitable doctrine of proprietary estoppel has had a significant impact on land law. Its role in the Irish land law system has not yet been conclusively determined. It is discussed briefly in the second half of this chapter.

I. TYPES OF LICENCES

LICENCE COUPLED WITH A PROPRIETARY INTEREST

This is a licence granted in order to facilitate the exercise of an easement or profit. For instance, in order for a landowner to exercise his proprietary right to cut turf from a bog on his neighbour's land, he will need a concurrent licence to walk across the land to get to the bog. This licence will last as long as the incorporeal hereditament does. It binds all third parties who are bound by the incorporeal hereditament. However, it is very limited in scope since it only exists to facilitate the use of the easement or profit.

BARE LICENCE

This is a licence which is not attached to any proprietary interest and has been given without consideration being received for it. It is a very weak form of licence and can be revoked by the grantor at any time on the giving of reasonable notice.

CONTRACTUAL LICENCE

This is a licence for which consideration has been given. Once consideration has been given, a contract between the licensee and licensor is regarded as being present, and the licence cannot be revoked by the licensor except in accordance with the terms of this contract. The court will grant an injunction to prevent its revocation by the licensor. However, a contractual licence does not bind third parties.

Originally the position was that as a licence was a personal right over land, the licensor could breach it with impunity. He could terminate the licence at any time and throw the licensee out and the licensee could do nothing to stop him. If the licensee had given consideration in return for the licence, the licensee could sue the licensor for damages for breach of contract. That was the only remedy available to the contractual licensee.

The case of *Winter Garden Theatre (London) Ltd v Millennium Productions Ltd* ([1948] A.C. 173) considerably increased the importance of contractual licences. This case established that, where a licensor attempted to throw a licensee off the land in breach of contract, the licensee could get an injunction to prevent the licensor from evicting him.

In the *Winter Garden* case the contract provided for a licence to hold plays and contracts in the defendant's theatre. It was held that the theatre owner could be stopped by injunction from revoking this licence in breach of contract. However, on the facts of the case the revocation was not in breach of contract.

Winter Garden had been anticipated in Ireland in *Whipp v Mackey* ([1927] I.R. 372) which stated that an injunction could be granted to prevent a licensor from wrongfully revoking a licence.

However, these cases merely took a more generous approach to the remedies available for breach of personal rights. They did not convert licences from personal into proprietary rights. This view was conclusively reaffirmed by the House of Lords in *Ashburn Anstalt v Arnold* ([1989] Ch. 1).

The House of Lords in *Ashburn* did indicate that a contractual licence might bind a third party in exceptional circumstances. However, it appears that such situations will be very limited as *Ashburn* made clear that even if the conveyance of land had been made expressly subject to the rights of the licensee, this would not be sufficient to justify the court in holding the purchaser bound by the licence.

ESTOPPEL LICENCE

This is a new and developing form of licence. It is a licence granted by a court in order to satisfy a proprietary estoppel. An estoppel licence may, if so directed by the court, bind third parties. It appears that the doctrine of proprietary estoppel may be utilised so as to create licences which actually bind third parties and are very close to proprietary rights.

II. PROPRIETARY ESTOPPEL

This is a doctrine whereby equity may take property rights away from somebody who has acted in an unconscionable manner and transfer them to the person who has suffered as a result of the unconscionability.

Jurisprudence has established that where one person incurs detriment in reliance on a belief that he has or will have an interest in land owned by another, the court may find that an estoppel has arisen. If the true owner of the land has encouraged this belief, or is aware of it and does not disabuse the mistaken person, he runs the risk of being estopped at a later date from pointing out that that person has no interest in the land.

An estoppel will not necessarily arise merely because the conditions in the above paragraph are satisfied. The overall principle is whether the true owner of land has acted unconscionably in the circumstances. The decision as to whether unconscionability is present depends to a large extent on the discretion of the judge.

Assuming estoppel is present, what remedies are available to the claimant? A court may order that the person who has suffered detriment should be paid compensation. It may grant him equitable ownership of the land under a constructive trust. Easements and leases have been granted where necessary to satisfy an estoppel. The court may even require the owner to convey the legal title in the land to the person who has incurred the detriment.

Another solution is to grant that person a licence over the land. Licences granted to satisfy an estoppel may, if directed, bind third parties. However, they are not full proprietary rights in so far as they cannot be transferred by the licensee.

The United Kingdom case of *Inwards v Baker* ([1965] 2 Q.B. 29) is an example of a situation in which an estoppel licence binding third parties was granted by the courts. In this case, a father suggested to a son that the son build a bungalow for himself on the father's land. On his death, the father left the land to his mistress. It was held that the father had given the son the belief that he could live on the land as long as he liked, and that the son had expended a considerable amount of money in building the bungalow in reliance on that belief. It was held that the son was entitled to remain on the land as long as he wished.

A similar principle was applied by Geoghegan J. in *Smyth v Halpin* (unreported, High Court, December 20, 1996). A son, deciding to get married, asked his father for a site on his land in order to build a house. His father's response was to the effect that the house would be left to his son following the death of his mother and that, as a result, he would not need two places. Instead, the father suggested that his son extend the family home rather than build an entirely new house. The family home was duly extended by the son in the belief that the entire house would ultimately be his. Following the father's death, it was discovered that the reversionary interest in the house had in fact been left by him to a third party, whereupon the son issued proceedings claiming an entitlement to have this interest transferred to him.

Geoghegan J. granted the relief sought by the plaintiff, stating that any reasonable person with knowledge of the family would have assumed that the intention at all material times was that the entire house would become the property of the plaintiff on the death of his parents. He did not believe that the plaintiff would ever have adopted his father's suggestion in relation to the extension of the house if it were not understood that he was to become the ultimate owner of the entire house.

Geoghegan J. stated further that, where an estoppel arose, it was for the court to say in what way the equity can be satisfied, and how best to protect it. In this case, the clear expectation on the part of the plaintiff was that he would have a fee simple in the entire house. The protection of the equity arising from his expenditure required that an order be made directing that there be a conveyance of the family home to him.

Smyth v Halpin was referred to approvingly by the Supreme Court in *F v JDF* (unreported, Supreme Court, McGuinness J., July 12, 2005; [2005] IESC 45), which, however, emphasised that to establish a beneficial interest in property arising from proprietary estoppel, there had to be a promise upon which the beneficiary was relying. In this case, an argument that a party to proceedings had an enforceable estoppel claim against his father failed due to lack of evidence of any actual promise, inducement or representation to that party by his father that he intended the husband to be the owner of the land.

A similar approach was taken by the same court in *William Bennett Construction Limited v Greene* (unreported, Supreme Court, Keane C.J., February 25, 2004; [2004] IESC 15) in which an estoppel claim to a wayleave failed due to the absence of any "clear and unambiguous promise or assurance" by the defendants.

Even a clear promise to transfer requires detrimental reliance in order to ground an estoppel. *In Bracken v Byrne* (unreported, High Court, Clarke J., March 11, 2005), an estoppel claim based on an oral promise to transfer land failed because the only manner in which the plaintiff had acted to her detriment in relation to the agreement was to obtain planning permission and obtain a quotation from a builder.

Leasehold Ownership

Leasehold ownership is the right to exclusive possession of land, normally for a limited period, under an agreement with its owner to hold as landlord and tenant.

The freehold owner of land, i.e. the person owning the fee simple in the land, grants possession of the land to someone else who is known as the tenant. The tenant has the right to exclusive possession of the land for the duration of the lease. The tenant is known as the leasehold owner of the land. The landlord is the freehold owner.

In most leases, the landlord has what is known as a reversion. When the period of the lease or tenancy comes to an end, he has a right to get the property back.

The creation of a lease is not the same as a transfer of freehold ownership. First, because a leasehold relationship gives rise to special rights on the part of the landlord, for example the right to forfeiture and the right to rent and, secondly, because the landlord usually gets the property back at the end of the period of the lease.

I. CREATION OF A LANDLORD-TENANT RELATIONSHIP

Under s.3 of the Landlord and Tenant (Amendment) (Ireland) Act 1860 (otherwise known as "Deasy's Act"), the landlord-tenant relationship in Ireland is deemed to be based on contract and to arise whenever there is an agreement to hold land from or under another in consideration of any rent.

AGREEMENT TO CREATE A LANDLORD-TENANT RELATIONSHIP

The concept of the landlord-tenant relationship is based on the notion of an agreement between two parties, the landlord and the tenant. They must first of all agree to create a landlord-tenant relationship and not any other kind of relationship, for example a licence. A licence would only confer a personal right to possession and not a proprietary right. It would not carry with it any of the statutory rights and obligations which attach to the landlord-tenant relationship.

Sometimes it may be difficult to distinguish an agreement for a licence from an agreement for a lease or tenancy. The leading Irish case on the lease-licence distinction is the judgment of the Supreme Court in *Irish Shell v*

LAND LAW

Costello ([1981] I.L.R.M. 66). In this case, an agreement conferring exclusive possession in return for periodic money payments was described as a licence but contained certain clauses more appropriate to a lease. For example, there was a clause prohibiting the tenant from assigning his interest. It was held by the Supreme Court that in deciding whether or not an agreement is a lease or a licence, a court should ignore the name-tags placed on the agreement by the parties and should instead look at the content of the agreement.

The grant of exclusive possession is an essential feature of a lease and if it is not present on the face of the agreement the agreement cannot be a lease and must be a licence. *Governors of National Maternity Hospital, Dublin v McGouran* ([1994] 1 I.L.R.M. 521) involved an agreement entered into by a hospital granting an individual the right to use part of the hospital as a coffee shop. The issue was whether the agreement was a lease or a licence. There was a clause in the agreement stating that the coffee shop licensee had no exclusive possession and that the hospital had the right to come on to the premises at any time they liked. On this basis the High Court held the agreement to be a licence.

Accordingly, one way in which to prevent an occupation agreement from giving rise to a tenancy would be to insert clauses providing for entry and/or relocation at the will of the owner. However, there should be some reality to the enforcement of these clauses since a court may refuse to recognise them if not genuine.

Rent is also a vital component of the landlord-tenant relationship and is specifically required by s.3 of Deasy's Act. In *Ó Siodhachain v O'Mahony* (unreported, High Court, October 31, 2002), Kearns J. held that a contract, argued to be a lease, was not a valid lease because it did not provide for rent.

One issue is whether "rent" in this context is confined to periodic money payments only so as not to include the performance of services. Deasy's Act itself leaves the question open to some extent by defining "rent" as "sum or return in the nature of rent".

One unresolved question in Irish law is whether exclusive possession and rent is sufficient, in itself, for a landlord-tenant relationship to subsist or whether or not there must also be a specific intention on the part of an owner and occupier to create a landlord-tenant relationship.

Although *Irish Shell v Costello* made clear that the owner of property could not preclude a lease simply by putting the word "licence" at the top of their agreement, the Supreme Court in that case continued to regard shared intention to create a landlord-tenant relationship as a necessary pre-requisite which must be satisfied, in addition to exclusive possession and rent, before a landlord-tenant relationship could be held to subsist.

Some doubt has been cast on the continued relevance of intention to create a landlord-tenant relationship by the decision of Peart J. in *Smith v Irish*

Rail (unreported, High Court, Peart J., October 9, 2002). This case involved an occupation agreement containing a specific provision stating that the parties did not intend to create a landlord-tenant relationship and that the relationship created thereby was one of personal privilege only. Peart J. held that, despite this clause, the agreement had created a lease, stating that the fact that the agreement gave exclusive possession to the occupier in return for the payment by him of periodic money sums effectively meant that it created a landlord-tenant relationship irrespective of the expressed intention of the parties.

In this regard, Peart J. followed the reasoning of the House of Lords in *Street v Mountford* ([1985] A.C. 809) to the effect that "the manufacture of a five-pronged implement for manual digging results in a fork, even if the manufacturer, unfamiliar with the English language, insists that he intended to make and has made a spade".

However, his approach in this case appears to conflict with that taken by the Supreme Court, both in *Irish Shell v Costello* and in the subsequent case of *Kenny Homes v Leonard* (unreported, Supreme Court, Lynch. J., June 18, 1998), in which an agreement conferring exclusive possession subject to a similar "personal privilege" clause was regarded as creating a licence only.

THE AGREEMENT MUST BE VALID UNDER CONTRACT LAW

An agreement to create a landlord-tenant relationship must be valid under contract law. There must be a valid offer and acceptance, and the agreement must not have been secured subject to duress, undue influence or mistake. Furthermore, it must not be too vague. If it is a lease for a term certain, the term must be certain. *Lace v Chantler* ([1944] 1 All E.R. 305) was a UK case where there was a lease for the duration of the war. This was held to be void for uncertainty.

THE NECESSARY WRITING REQUIREMENTS MUST BE FULFILLED

Finally, there are certain writing requirements which must be fulfilled in order to create a landlord-tenant relationship. Unless the lease is for year-to-year or any lesser period, it has to be in writing under Deasy's Act. Otherwise it cannot be a valid lease at common law.

The Deasy's Act writing requirement does not apply to yearly, weekly or monthly tenancies. It is an unresolved issue whether it applies to a lease for one year certain. Case law is divided on the issue of whether a tenancy for one year certain is for a lesser period than a yearly tenancy. In *Wright v Tracey* ((1874) 8 I.R.C.L. 478) it was held that a tenancy for one year certain was not less than a tenancy from year-to-year and as such needed to be in writing.

However, there has been criticism of this case in the decisions of *Jameson v Squire* ([1948] I.R. 153) and *Bernays v Prosser* ([1963] 2 All E.R. 321).

What happens if an agreement fails to satisfy the necessary writing requirements under Deasy's Act? In such case it may be possible to enforce it in equity as an agreement to create a lease. This is known as the principle in *Walsh v Lonsdale* ((1882) 21 Ch D 9). In order to do this, it is necessary to show either the fulfilment of writing requirements sufficient to satisfy the Statute of Frauds or an act of part performance.

Writing requirements under the Statute of Frauds are slightly different from writing requirements under Deasy's Act. For example, under the Statute of Frauds the note in writing need not be made at the same time as the oral agreement is concluded. Under Deasy's Act, on the other hand, the note in writing must be contemporaneous with the oral agreement. Secondly, under the Statute of Frauds, the note in writing only has to be signed by the party to be charged on it. In contrast, under Deasy's Act the note in writing has to be signed by the landlord. Thirdly, under the Statute of Frauds an agent who signs does not have to have written authorisation.

Part performance occurs in the following situations: when the tenant goes into possession and pays rent or expends money on improvements. It may be difficult to show part performance when a previous tenant continues in possession under a new lease which is not in writing. Some variation in the payment of rent may suffice. In *McCausland v Murphy* ((1881) 9 L.R. Ir. 9), the tenant had taken possession of and carried out alterations to the property, which were held to be sufficient acts of part performance.

What happens if there is neither a legal nor an equitable lease because the writing formalities are not fulfilled and there is no part performance? In this situation the original agreement cannot take effect. If the tenant goes into possession and pays rent there may be a periodic tenancy, depending on the method used for paying the rent.

If the tenant goes into possession with the consent of the landlord and does not pay rent he is a tenant at will. A tenant at will becomes an adverse possessor after one year.

II. Types of Landlord-Tenant Relationships

Traditionally, the law distinguished between landlord-tenant relationships based on whether or not they were fixed-term or periodic.

A fixed-term lease is a lease for a definite period, e.g. 21 years. Under Deasy's Act 1860, it was possible to create a lease forever and such leases, if created before December 1, 2009, still continue in existence (although the facility to create new leases forever has now been removed by s.12 of the Land and Conveyancing Law Reform Act 2009).

A periodic tenancy, on the other hand, is a tenancy for a particular period, e.g. a week, a month or a year. It will be automatically renewed at the end of the period unless either party demonstrates their intention to terminate it by serving a notice to quit.

There are two other types of relationship which are sometimes characterised as landlord-tenant relationships but which in strict legal terms fall outside that category. A tenancy at will arises when a fixed-term lease comes to an end and the tenant over holds with the consent of the landlord but without paying regular rent. A tenancy at sufferance arises when a lease or tenancy comes to an end and the tenant stays on in the premises without the assent or dissent of the landlord.

The enactment of the Residential Tenancies Act 2004 (the "2004 Act") has introduced a new distinction into landlord and tenant law, namely a distinction between:

(i)   leases and tenancies of residential property falling within the scope of the 2004 Act (which includes most residential property) and

(ii) other leases and tenancies.

The 2004 Act serves as a one-stop shop for leases and tenancies falling within its scope, with disputes in relation to same being determined by the Private Residential Tenancies Board rather than by the courts.

Leases and tenancies falling outside the 2004 Act, on the other hand, continue to be regulated by the old law, which is a mixture of the common law, Deasy's Act, the Landlord and Tenant (Amendment) Act 1980 and other miscellaneous statutory provisions.

It is proposed to first consider the rules applicable to landlord-tenant obligations, termination and statutory rights under the 2004 Act before going on to consider separately the rules applicable to tenancies falling outside the scope of that Act.

III. Landlord-Tenant Relationships Falling within the Residential Tenancies Act 2004

All tenancies of residential property or "dwellings" apart from a number of tenancies specifically excluded by s.3(2) fall within the scope of the 2004 Act.

The relatively small category of residential properties excluded from the scope of the 2004 Act by s.3(2) as amended by s.100 of the Housing

(Miscellaneous Provisions) Act 2009 include holiday and shared-ownership lettings, dwellings let by or to public authorities or by or to certain bodies approved for social housing purposes, as well as dwellings subject to continuing control under the Housing (Private Rented Dwellings) Act 1982 or used wholly or partly for the purpose of carrying on business or held under tenancies for more than 35 years.

Dwellings where the occupier is entitled to buy out the fee simple under the Landlord and Tenant (Ground Rents) Acts 1967–2005 or in which the owner or certain members of his family also reside are similarly excluded. However, most lettings of privately-owned rented accommodation fall within the scope of the 2004 Act which substantially changes the law applicable to such lettings.

The most significant change is that disputes regarding these tenancies are no longer dealt with by means of courts system. Section 182 of the 2004 Act states that:

> proceedings may not be instituted in any court in respect of a residential tenancy dispute unless one of the following reliefs is being claimed in the proceedings
> (a) damages of an amount of more than 20,000 Euros
> (b) recovery of arrears of rent, or other charges, or both, of an amount of more than 60,000 Euros.

Instead, all such disputes must be referred to the Private Residential Tenancies Board (the "Board"). The procedure before the Board, as set out in Pt 6 of the 2004 Act, is as follows: it can invite parties to submit to mediation, if they both consent this can be done. If there is no agreement to refer to mediation, the Board will appoint an adjudicator. It is possible to appeal the determination of the adjudicator to the Tenancy Tribunal which is a three-person body appointed by the Board. An appeal on a point of law only to the High Court lies from the determination of the Tenancy Tribunal. It is also possible to make an application to the Circuit Court to enforce determination orders made by the mediator, the adjudicator or the Tenancy Tribunal, which have not been obeyed.

i) Obligations of landlords and tenants under residential tenancies

Part 2 of the 2004 Act recognises new landlord and tenant obligations, which are to apply irrespective of whether the tenancy agreement is oral or written, periodic or fixed-term.

Under s.12 of the 2004 Act, the landlord is under an on-going duty of repair in relation to both the structure and the interior of the dwelling; to insure against destruction and liability; to repay any deposit paid by the tenant unless there has been a failure to pay rent or the tenant has caused damage to the dwelling; to notify the tenant of the name of the person authorised to act on his behalf in relation to the tenancy; and to detail to the tenant how he or his authorised agent can be contacted.

The landlord also has a duty not to penalise the tenant for enforcing his rights under the 2004 Act and a duty to third parties to enforce the obligations of the tenant.

Under s.16 the tenant is under a duty to pay the rent and also to pay any charges or taxes required by the tenancy agreement. The tenant is also under a duty not to act/fail to act in such a way as to prevent the landlord's statutory obligations in relation to the dwelling from being complied with.

The tenant is also under a duty to allow the landlord access to the premises at reasonable intervals for the purpose of inspecting the dwelling; to notify the landlord of any defect in the dwelling that requires repair; to provide the landlord with reasonable access for the purpose of carrying out these works; and not to do any act that would cause a deterioration in the condition the dwelling was in at the commencement of the tenancy (but normal wear and tear is excepted from this).

In addition, the tenant is under a duty not to behave or allow others in the dwelling to behave in an antisocial manner or to act in a way which might invalidate insurance policy or cause an increase in the landlord's insurance premium. Nor can a tenant assign or sublet without written consent of the landlord; however, under s.186 of the 2004 Act such tenant can terminate the tenancy immediately if the landlord's consent to an assignment or subletting is withheld.

ii) STATUTORY RIGHTS OF TENANTS HOLDING UNDER RESIDENTIAL TENANCIES

One of the most important aspects of the 2004 Act is Pt 4 of the Act which deals with the tenant's statutory right to a Part 4 tenancy, which comes into existence whenever a tenant has been in occupation for more than six months after the date of coming into effect of the 2004 Act without a valid notice of termination having been served on him.

In such case, s.28(2) provides that the tenant becomes entitled to Part 4 protection (described as a "Part 4 tenancy") for a further three-and-a-half years during which time his tenancy can only be determined by the landlord pursuant to the following grounds in s.34 of the 2004 Act:

- Where the tenant has been in breach of his or her obligations in relation to the tenancy, and has failed to remedy such breach within a reasonable time following notification of same.

- Where the dwelling the subject of the tenancy "is no longer suitable to the accommodation needs of the tenant and of any persons residing with him or her having regard to the number of bed spaces contained in the dwelling and the size and composition of the occupying household".

- Where the landlord wishes to enter into "an enforceable agreement for the transfer to another, for full consideration, of the whole of his or her interest in the dwelling" within three months of the termination of the Part 4 tenancy.

- Where the landlord requires the dwelling the subject of the tenancy for his or her own occupation or for the occupation by a member of his or her family for a period of at least six months.

- Where the landlord intends to substantially refurbish or renovate the dwelling or the property containing same in a way which requires the dwelling to be vacated or if he intends to change the use of the dwelling.

Section 40 provides that a second or further Part 4 tenancy will automatically arise on the expiration of the statutory protection specified in s.28(2) in the event of a notice of termination not having been served prior to this date.

However, s.42(1) goes on to provide that this further Part 4 tenancy may be terminated by the service of a notice of termination within six months of its commencement without having to show cause. The period of notice in this case should not be less than 112 days, unless the tenant is in breach, in which case the shorter period specified in s.67 applies. If such notice of termination is not served within this six-month period, the Part 4 tenancy will become absolute and continue for a further three-and-a-half years and the same process will be repeated on its determination.

iii) TERMINATION OF RESIDENTIAL TENANCIES

In addition, Pt 5 of the 2004 Act provides a completely new method of terminating residential tenancies. All residential tenancies, irrespective of whether or not they are subject to Part 4 protection, must be determined by notice of termination, all other methods of termination (e.g. forfeiture, notice to quit) being abolished.

Section 62 goes on to set out the substantive requirements which must be satisfied in respect of every notice of termination. This section is quite specific and recent decisions of the Residential Tenancies Tribunal indicate that non-compliance with any part of same will invalidate the termination. A valid notice of termination must be in writing and signed by the party terminating the tenancy. The date of service must be specified thereon. It should be "in such form, if any, as may be prescribed".

In addition, it should specify the date on which the tenancy will terminate (the termination date). This date will depend on the appropriate notice period which must be given. The widely varying notice periods for termination of residential tenancies set out in ss.66–68 of the 2004 Act will be discussed below.

Finally, all notices of termination must contain a statement to the effect that any issue as to the validity of the notice or the right of the landlord or tenant, as appropriate, to serve it must be referred to the Private Residential Tenancies Board under Pt 6 of the 2004 Act within 28 days from the date of receipt of same.

Where the termination is by the landlord, additional requirements apply. The Notice must specifically state the date "on or before which ... the tenant must vacate possession of the dwelling concerned". Presumably this will be the same as the termination date. Where it is, the notice must indicate that the tenant has the whole of the 24 hours of the termination date to vacate possession. If "the duration of the tenancy is a period of more than 6 months", the notice must also state the reason for the termination.

Ascertaining the appropriate notice period in respect of a tenancy is crucial. If this is not done, the danger is that the termination date specified on the notice may be too early and held to be incorrect. Since giving an excessive period of notice does not automatically invalidate a notice of termination, it is better to err on the side of a late, rather than an early, termination date. The one exception is in the case of tenancies for less than six months, where s.65(4) provides that a notice period of more than 70 days renders the notice of termination invalid.

When ascertaining the applicable notice periods in the case of termination by a landlord, it is important to distinguish between termination in situations where the tenant has been in breach of his obligations under the tenancy (s.67) and other types of termination (s.66).

Where the tenant's breach is due to certain types of antisocial behaviour, or conduct "threatening to the fabric of the dwelling or the property containing the dwelling", only seven days' notice needs to be given in order to terminate his tenancy. In respect of most other breaches of obligation by the tenant, the appropriate notice period is 28 days. Under s.34, where the landlord is exercising his right to terminate a Part 4 tenancy early on account of breach by the tenant, the tenant must first be informed of the breach and given the opportunity to remedy same. This does not apply to terminations for breach of obligation outside the context of a Part 4 tenancy.

Special rules apply in relation to termination for non-payment of rent. In this case, s.67(3) provided that before the notice of termination can be served it must be shown that the tenant was notified in writing of the amount of rent due at least 14 days previous to the proposed date of service of the notice and failed to pay same. Where the tenant is a Part 4 tenant, Laffoy J. in *Canty v Private Residential Tenancies Board* (High Court, August 8, 2007) held that a further notice pursuant to s.34, Condition 1 must also be served after the expiry of the rent notification before a valid notice of termination can issue.

The notice periods for termination by the landlord where there has been no breach of obligations on the part of the tenant are set out in s.66, Table 1 of the 2004 Act and vary depending on the duration of the tenancy from the date of coming into effect of the 2004 Act.

If the tenancy has been in existence for less than six months after September 2004, then the minimum notice period is 28 days and the maximum notice period is 70 days. In the case of tenancies which have been in existence for more than six months after the coming into effect of the 2004 Act, there is no maximum notice period, but the minimum notice given by the landlord must be 35 days in the case of a tenancy which has lasted more than six months but less than one year, 42 days in the case of a tenancy more than one year but less than two years, 56 days in the case of a tenancy more than two years but less than three years, 84 days in the case of a tenancy more than three years but less than four years and 112 days in the case of a tenancy of four years or more.

However, it is important to note that the observation of the above notice periods does not necessarily mean the termination is valid. The scope for termination by the landlord where there has been no breach of obligations on the part of the tenant is generally very limited. First, s.58(3) makes clear that a notice of termination cannot be used to determine a fixed-term lease early in the absence of a breach of covenant by the tenant. Even where there is no fixed-term lease, or where same has expired, the service of a notice of termination may be precluded under s.33 by the fact that a statutory tenancy under Pt 4 of the 2004 Act has arisen in favour of the tenant.

The notice periods applicable in relation to termination by a tenant are set out in s.66, Table 2 and s.68. Section 68 provides for termination by the tenant on seven days' notice where the landlord has engaged in behaviour which poses an imminent danger of death or serious injury or imminent danger to the fabric of the dwelling or the property containing same. It also provides for a notice period of 28 days where the landlord has been in breach of his obligations under the lease, has been notified of same by the tenant, and has failed to remedy same within a reasonable time.

The notice periods applicable in respect of termination by a tenant in the absence of any breach by the landlord are set out in Table 2 of s.66. Where the tenancy has been in existence for less than six months after the coming into effect of the 2004 Act, the minimum notice period is 28 days and the maximum notice period is 70 days. In the case of tenancies which have lasted for six months or more after the coming into effect of the 2004 Act, there is no maximum notice period and the minimum notice period varies from 35 days (in the case of tenancies of six or more months but less than a year) to 56 days (in the case of tenancies of two or more years).

It should be noted that a tenant cannot serve a notice of termination to cut short a fixed-term lease, unless a breach on the part of the landlord can be shown or unless the landlord has refused his consent to an assignment or subletting. However, a tenant is entitled to determine a Part 4 tenancy by serving a notice of termination at any time without cause. This applies both to original and subsequent Part 4 tenancies and contrasts with the landlord's position as set out in s.33 of the 2004 Act and detailed above.

IV. Leasehold Arrangements Falling Outside the Residential Tenancies Act 2004

The law in relation to obligations of landlord and tenant, termination and statutory landlord and tenant rights under leasehold arrangements falling outside the Residential Tenancies Act 2004 is governed by a mixture of common law, Deasy's Act 1860 and the Landlord and Tenant (Amendment) Act 1980 (the "1980 Act").

i) Obligations of landlords and tenants

Subject to certain amendments effected by ss.65–68 of the 1980 Act, the obligations of landlord and tenant in such arrangements are governed by the terms of the agreement between the parties. Two features always present in such arrangements are an obligation on the part of the landlord to allow the tenant exclusive possession and an obligation on the part of the tenant to pay rent.

The lease or tenancy may contain a rent review provision providing for an increase in the rent after a certain period. Section 132 of the Land and Conveyancing Law Reform Act 2009 provides that a rent review clause in a commercial lease entered into on or after February 14, 2010 shall be construed as allowing the reviewed rent to be less than the amount previously payable, notwithstanding any provision to the contrary in the lease, or agreement for the lease. The section has no effect on upwards-only rent review clauses in leases which pre-date February 14, 2010, which continue to apply.

The allocation of repair obligations in non-residential landlord tenant arrangements normally depends on the terms of the agreement between the parties. Where a written lease is silent on the question of repair, s.42 of Deasy's Act 1860 imposes an implied obligation on the tenant to keep premises in good and substantial repair and condition. This applies only to the extent that it is not contradicted in whole or in part by an express provision to the contrary in the lease.

The covenant implied by s.42 is particularly wide-ranging because it is a covenant "to keep" in repair. In *Groome v Fodhla Printing Co. Ltd* ([1943] I.R. 380), the Supreme Court held that such a covenant involved an obligation to put premises into good repair if they were not in good repair at the commencement of the lease. In this case there was a problem with the roof of the premises, which it was held that the tenant was obliged to fix despite the fact that it pre-dated the grant of the lease.

This approach may be contrasted with that taken in *Údarás na Gaeltachta v Uisce Glan Teoranta* (High Court, O'Neill J., March 13, 2007; [2007] IEHC 95) in which O'Neill J. took the view that a covenant "to repair" (as opposed to a covenant "to keep in" repair) did not oblige a tenant to carry out any works improving premises beyond their state of repair at the time that the property was demised to them.

Groome was also distinguished in *Whelan v Madigan* ([1978] I.L.R.M. 136) which involved a provision in a lease obliging the tenant to keep the interior only of the flat in good condition. It was held that this did not oblige a tenant to remedy structural defects, even where these defects (in that case, lack of adequate damp proofing) were affecting the interior of the premises.

Express covenants restricting the use to which the property may be put, and/or restricting assignment or subletting are also common in leases. However, such covenants (along with tenant repair covenants) are subject to statutory modification by the 1980 Act when contained in leases of tenements.

A tenement is a property which consists wholly or partly of buildings, with any part of the property not covered by buildings being merely subsidiary and ancillary to the buildings. Consequently, the term applies mainly to urban land, e.g. a house with a garden would be included in the definition because the garden could be said to be ancillary to the house.

Section 65 of the 1980 Act is a very important provision which significantly modifies the tenant's liability to pay damages for breach of a repair covenant. It only applies to tenements. It does not limit the landlord's right to forfeiture for breach of a repairing covenant.

Section 65 is divided into subss.(2) and (3). Subsection (2) restricts the amount of damages recoverable. It provides that the damages recoverable by the landlord from the tenant cannot exceed the amount by which the value of the lessor's reversion has been diminished. Subsection (3) limits the circumstances in which damages may be recoverable. It provides that damages are not recoverable from the tenant for breach of a repairing covenant in three situations:

(a) Where repair is physically impossible.
(b) Where repair would involve disproportionate expenditure in relation to the value of the tenement.
(c) Where the tenement could not be profitably used on repair.

However, there is also an important qualification to subs.(3); it does not apply, even in the three situations detailed above, if the want of repair is due wholly or substantially to wilful damage or wilful waste committed by the lessee. Note that this qualification only applies to subs.(3) and not subs.(2).

Section 66 of the 1980 Act, which again only applies to tenements, relates to covenants restricting or prohibiting assignment or subletting. It provides that if a landlord uses these covenants to refuse consent to an assignment or subletting he must be shown to be acting reasonably. Doubts about the solvency of the proposed assignee constitute a reasonable ground for refusing consent.

In *Cregan and Another v Taviri Ltd* (High Court, Charleton J., May 30, 2008), Charleton J. held that it was not unreasonable, in circumstances where a lease contained a guarantee for the landlord to make any assignment conditional on one of the existing guarantors remaining in place to ensure the new lessee would continue to perform the obligations that had been fulfilled up to that point.

In *Meagher & Or v Luke J. Healy Pharmacy Limited* ([2010] IEHC 40) the Supreme Court took the view that there was no basis, under s.66 or otherwise, for awarding damages to a tenant who had suffered the loss of an assignee by reason of a landlord's refusal of consent to an assignment, even where that refusal was unreasonable, unless the landlord had specifically covenanted, in the landlord covenant section of the lease, not to unreasonably refuse consent.

Section 67 of the 1980 Act relates to covenants restricting the use to which the land may be put by the tenant. As with ss.65 and 66, it only applies to tenements. As with s.66, it provides that a landlord may not invoke such covenants unreasonably. There are a number of cases defining unreasonable-ness in the context of s.67.

In *Rice v Dublin Corporation* ([1947] I.R. 425) there was a covenant in the lease of a tenement prohibiting the premises from being used as a pub or a brothel. It was held on the facts that the landlord was acting unreasonably in refusing his consent to the use of the premises as a pub. There was no evidence that Dublin Corporation had a policy as to the correct number of licensed premises in that neighbourhood. In the absence of a clear policy, refusal of consent was unreasonable. Limiting the number of pubs in an area might be reasonable, but excluding them altogether was not.

However, in contrast with *Rice* there are a number of cases relating to covenants restricting user of units in shopping centres. In all these cases a landlord's refusal of consent to a change in user was held reasonable on the ground of estate management.

In *Greene Property v Shalaine Modes* ([1978] 1 I.L.R.M. 222) it was a term of a lease of a unit in a shopping centre that the premises would be used as a hardware store. User was changed to a women's boutique without objection from the landlord, and then to a toy shop. The owner of another toy shop within the centre objected, which prompted the landlord to refuse his consent to the change of use. It was held that the landlord was reasonable in refusing his consent. The lessor in a shopping centre has a financial interest in maintaining a good mix of shops. The more attractive the shopping centre, the higher the rents he could charge.

This approach was replicated in *Wanze Properties (Ireland) Ltd v Mastertron Ltd* ([1992] I.L.R.M. 746). Here the lessor objected to the opening of a Chinese takeaway in the premises which were the subject of the lease. He argued that the Chinese takeaway would have dead frontage which was a disadvantage in a shopping centre. He also pointed out that such a business operated mainly in the evening so that it was closed when most of the shops in the centre were open, and open when they were closed. His refusal of consent was held reasonable.

This can be contrasted with the decision of Clarke J. in *Dunnes Stores (Ilac Centre) Ltd v Irish Life Assurance PLC* ([2008] IEHC 114) which involved a claim by Dunnes, the lessee of a shop unit in the Ilac Centre, that its landlord was acting unreasonably in refusing consent for the change of part of the unit to a food hall. The basis of the landlord's refusal, as set out in correspondence, was that such user would conflict with their vision for the shopping centre as a primary retail fashion area. However, the lease itself provided that in deciding whether or not to grant consent to a change of user, the landlord would have regard to the need for diversity within the centre. Clarke J. held that the landlord had acted unreasonably by failing to comply with its expressly assumed obligation under the lease to take account of the need for diversity; in addition, its refusal of consent was at least partly motivated by a desire to pressurise Dunnes into surrendering the unit.

ii) TERMINATION OF NON-RESIDENTIAL TENANCIES

Termination of non-residential tenancies varies depending on whether or not they are fixed-term or periodic in nature.

A fixed-term lease comes to an end by expiry when the term of the lease runs out. Additionally, the Statute of Limitations 1957 provides that a tenancy at will automatically expires after one year and that a tenancy from year to year which is not in writing will end at the end of the first year.

A fixed-term lease may come to an end before its allocated term by surrender, merger or forfeiture.

Surrender occurs when the tenant under a fixed-term lease conveys his leasehold interest back to the landlord before the expiry of the lease. For a surrender to be valid, it ought to satisfy s.7 of Deasy's Act by being a note in writing signed by the tenant. Sometimes surrender will be implied from the acts of the parties in cases where s.7 is not satisfied. It is important to remember that a lessee does not have an automatic right to surrender. He must be given that right by statute, by the lease, or by the agreement of the landlord.

Merger occurs when the leasehold and freehold interest become vested in either the tenant or a third party. Before merger can occur, there must be an additional intention on the part of the new owner to merge the two estates. This is demonstrated by the case of *Craig v Greer* ([1899] 1 I.R. 258). Here a sub-lease provided that the sub-lessees were bound by covenants contained in the head lease. The sub-lessor subsequently acquired the estate of the head lessor. It was argued that this brought about a merger which destroyed his rights under the sub-lease and the covenants, and so they no longer bound the sub-lessees. The court held that it had not been the intention of the sub-lessor to bring about a merger, as such a merger would have destroyed his rights under the sub-lease.

The contractual doctrine of frustration also applies to leases. In the context of a lease, destruction of a house is probably not enough to terminate a lease. In order for the contract to be frustrated, the actual land would have to be destroyed, e.g. by subsidence into the sea. There is a statutory frustration clause contained in s.40 of Deasy's Act. Where a dwelling house is destroyed by fire or inevitable accident, the tenant may surrender the lease. However, this clause is of little practical importance because it only applies if the lease does not contain an express covenant to repair. Most leases contain such a covenant.

Fixed-term landlord-tenant relationships may additionally be terminated early by the landlord by forfeiture for breach of covenant. In order for this to occur, there must either be an express forfeiture clause in the agreement expressly providing that the landlord has the right to forfeit for the breach of covenant or alternatively the covenant must be a condition of the lease. A covenant will normally be regarded as a condition if it is introduced by wording such as "on condition that" or "provided that". All properly drafted written leases and tenancies contain an express forfeiture clause.

In addition, before forfeiting, it may be necessary to serve a forfeiture notice on the tenant under s.14 of the Conveyancing Act 1881. A forfeiture notice is not necessary where the covenant breached is one relating to the non-payment of rent. In such cases the only obligation on the landlord is to comply with the common law and make a demand for the rent. The need for a demand for the rent may be excluded by the terms of the lease.

However, there can be no exclusion of the obligation to serve a forfeiture notice under s.14 when forfeiting for all breaches other than the non-payment of rent. In such case, the notice must specify the breach, and request the tenant to remedy same within a specified time, which should be a reasonable time in the circumstances. It must also warn the tenant that if the breach is not remedied within that period, forfeiture will be effected.

The service of the forfeiture notice does not itself determine the lease. In order for this to occur there would have to be an act of forfeiture which could either be the initiation of legal proceedings seeking possession of the premises or an act of physical re-entry. No act other than the above can constitute a valid act of forfeiture. In *Bank of Ireland v Lady Lisa Ireland Ltd* ([1993] I.L.R.M. 235), O Hanlon J. held that the service of a notice which indicated that the lessor was exercising its right to determine the lease and demanding possession did not in itself constitute a sufficient act of forfeiture, unless combined with one of the above methods.

Even if the above grounds are satisfied, forfeiture may still be denied under the equitable remedy of relief against forfeiture, or by some statutory provision, for example under s.27 of the Landlord and Tenant (Ground Rents) (No. 2) Act 1978 which provides that a landlord cannot forfeit a lease of a dwelling house for non-payment of rent where the tenant has the right to acquire the fee simple under the Ground Rents Acts 1967–2005.

In addition, even if the court finds the tenant was liable to pay the rent it may still decide to give him relief against forfeiture, particularly in cases where the forfeiture is based on the non-payment of money. Kennedy C.J. in *Whipp v Mackey* ([1927] I.R. 372) emphasised that such relief is a matter for exercise of judicial discretion but that a very strong case should be made for the granting of relief where the forfeiture is based solely on non-payment of a sum of money, which the tenant is now in a position to pay and no injury has resulted from the delay in payment or only such injury as payment of interest, plus costs, would be full compensation.

The application of *Whipp v Mackey* to commercial leases was questioned by the Supreme Court in *Cue Club Ltd v Navaro Ltd* (unreported, Supreme Court, Murphy J., October 23, 1996) where it recognised that the commercial viability of a shopping centre might well depend on all the tenants paying their rents and service charges promptly. The view was expressed by the Supreme Court in that case that the *Whipp v Mackey* principle would not necessarily apply in respect of substantial commercial transactions where the lessor and lessee could be said to be on equal terms.

Campus and Stadium Development v Dublin Waterworld ([2005] IEHC 334) represents a further move away from the traditional approach. Gilligan J. refused to grant relief to a tenant of valuable commercial premises who had willfully failed to comply with substantial financial obligations and to disclose important information to the landlord necessary to enable the landlord to assess the financial returns due to him on the premises. A tenant of high-rent commercial premises can no longer be guaranteed relief against forfeiture in a situation where it has wilfully and consistently disregarded its obligations.

A further (but rarely used) method for determining a fixed-term lease is the statutory termination method set out in s.52 of Deasy's Act which allows a landlord to initiate court proceedings to get the tenant out, provided that a year's rent is due and the tenancy is for a year or more. The lessee can obtain a stay of the proceedings by producing rent. Even after proceedings have been completed and the lessee has been ejected, he may apply for an order of restitution. He must do this within a period of six months. This means that the lessor cannot sell the premises for six months and consequently this makes s.52 relatively ineffective.

Periodic tenancies (including periodic tenancies arising by over holding following the expiry of a fixed-term lease) continue indefinitely and will normally only end if either the landlord or the tenant serves a notice to quit. Although in theory periodic tenancies could also be determined by surrender, merger or possibly even forfeiture, notice to quit remains the most common way of determining such tenancies.

A document will satisfy the definition of a notice to quit if it amounts to a clear and unambiguous communication of an intention to end the tenancy at the determination of a specified period. Once the period has come to an end, the tenancy determines.

It is preferable that the notice to quit should be in writing, but this is not compulsory. Furthermore, extra requirements may have to be satisfied if the agreement of tenancy provides that any notice to quit should be in a specified form. Statute further requires that a notice to quit in relation to agricultural land should be in writing and signed, and that a notice to quit residential accommodation must be in writing and delivered at least four weeks in advance of the date on which the notice period runs out.

One week's notice is necessary to end a weekly tenancy. At least one month's notice must be given to end a monthly tenancy. To end a yearly tenancy a half-year's (183 days) notice is needed. Special notice periods apply to agricultural lettings.

These periods are often extended in practice, because of rules relating to expiry of the notice. A notice to quit must expire at the end of a period of tenancy in order to be valid. Take the example of a weekly tenancy which started on a Monday. In a situation where the landlord decides on a Wednesday to get rid of his tenant, it is not permissible for him merely to give the tenant notice that day and expect him to have left the premises by the following Wednesday. The notice to quit must give at least a week's notice and be framed so as to expire on the last day of the period of tenancy. Thus, even if he serves on a Wednesday, time does not begin to run until the following Monday and the tenant does not have to leave until Monday week (or Monday four weeks if he has a residential tenancy).

For this reason, it is important to know the exact date on which the tenancy commenced. If this is not known, it is best to look at the gale day, which is the day on which the rent is paid. In *Lynch v Dolan* ([1973] I.R. 319) there was a weekly tenancy. The date of commencement of the tenancy was not known, but the rent was paid on a Friday. So notice to quit served on a Friday to quit on the next Friday was acceptable. If the commencement of a yearly tenancy is not known, there is a presumption that it commences on the last gale day of any calendar year.

iii) STATUTORY RIGHTS

The most important of the statutory rights available to non-residential tenants is the right to a new tenancy under Pt II of the 1980 Act. This right only applies in respect of tenements as defined above in the context of discussion of ss.65–68 of the 1980 Act. In addition to the land being a tenement, the tenant claiming the right must show the existence of one of three alternative equities:

The first of these equities, business equity, arises where there has been continuous occupation of the premises as a business by the tenant or their predecessors in title (defined as previous tenants under the same lease or tenancy or any lease or tenancy of which the most recent lease or tenancy may be deemed to be a continuation or renewal) for five years prior to the determination of the lease or tenancy (three years if the lease or tenancy was entered into before August 10, 1994). The term "business" includes social, cultural, sporting activities, or the practice of a profession, and is not necessarily confined to activities carried on for reward.

Alternatively, a tenant could claim a new tenancy on the basis of long user equity (occupation for 20 years prior to the determination of the lease or tenancy by the tenant or their predecessors in title as defined above) or improvement equity, which applies where half or more of the letting value of the tenement, at the date of determination of the lease or tenancy, is attributable to improvements carried out by the tenant or their predecessors in title, for which they would be entitled to be compensated under Pt IV of the 1980 Act.

Certain types of tenants (tenants of State property and non-business tenants of local authority property) are excluded from claiming rights under Pt II of the 1980 Act. In addition, there are certain grounds set out in s.17 of the 1980 Act whereby the right to a new tenancy under Pt II may legitimately be refused even where the above conditions are fulfilled.

Among the grounds listed in s.17(1) are where the tenancy has been terminated for non-payment of rent or breach of covenant or if there is other good and sufficient reason, attributable to the misconduct of the tenant, for denying a new tenancy.

It can be difficult to preclude a tenant from getting a new tenancy on this basis, even where there has been misbehavior or breach of covenant. In *Genport Ltd v Crofter Properties Ltd* (High Court, McGovern J., February 20, 2008), McGovern J. refused to deny a tenant a new tenancy, even where there had been prolonged and persistent breaches of covenant by the tenant during the life of the tenancy, stating that in determining whether the landlord had "good and sufficient reason" for refusing to grant a new tenancy, s.17 entitled the court to have "regard to all the circumstances of the case" and that in that case the landlord had also been in breach, which had contributed at least in part to the tenant's breaches.

Originally, there was no facility for contracting out of the right to a new tenancy under Pt II of the 1980 Act. However, s.47 of the Civil Law (Miscellaneous Provisions) Act 2008 extended s.17(1) of the 1980 Act to provide that a tenant who would otherwise be entitled to a new tenancy on the basis of business equity would be denied such a right where they had previously renounced same in writing following independent legal advice.

In addition to the restrictions on the right to a new tenancy set out in s.17(1) (as extended), there are also additional provisions contained in s.17(2) of the 1980 Act whereby a tenant's right to a new tenancy may be restricted where the landlord is carrying out rebuilding or reconstruction, incorporating the property in a scheme of development or simply requires possession of same on the basis of good estate management. However, in contrast to the restrictions in s.17(1), a landlord who relies on s.17(2) to deny a tenant a new tenancy will have to pay that tenant compensation for disturbance under Pt IV of the 1980 Act.

iv) THE EXTENT OF THE RIGHT

If the tenant satisfies the criteria for the grant of a new tenancy, the court fixes the terms of the new tenancy. It should be 35 years or less in duration, and if the tenancy arises through business equity it should be for 20 years or less. The rent fixed is the gross rent, namely that rent which a willing lessee would give and a willing lessor would take on the basis of vacant possession.

Tenants may, in exceptional cases, be entitled to buy out the fee simple under the Landlord and Tenant (Ground Rents) Acts 1967–2005 for a nominal sum in circumstances where they satisfy the conditions in the Landlord and Tenant (Ground Rents) (No. 2) Act 1978. The relevant sections of that Act are ss.9 and 10 (in the case of tenants holding under a fixed-term lease) and s.15 (in the case of yearly tenants not holding under temporary convenience lettings or in consideration of an office, appointment or employment).

Generally these provisions require that there be buildings on the property and that these buildings be erected by the tenant or their predecessors in title. Where the lease is for a term of 50 years or more at a rent less than the rateable valuation there may be an entitlement to acquire the fee simple without having to prove erection of the buildings; however, such entitlement may be defeated if the landlord proves that the buildings have been erected by him or his predecessors in title.

There are also a number of additional alternative criteria set out at s.10 Conditions 3–7 of the 1978 (No. 2) Act applicable to tenants holding under fixed-term leases only. The entitlement to acquire the fee simple is confined to the buildings themselves and land subsidiary and ancillary thereto; land also forming part of the lease or tenancy but not subsidiary and ancillary to the buildings should be severed from the application.

Fixed-term tenants who qualify under s.9 of the Landlord and Tenant (Ground Rents) (No.2) Act 1978 are also entitled to claim in the alternative a reversionary lease under Pt III of the 1980 Act. A reversionary lease is a lease for a very long time (99 years), at a low rent, which is automatically renewable.

Most such tenants, however, prefer, where possible, to buy out the landlord's interest and determine the lease; one advantage of a reversionary lease claim, however, is that unlike a claim to buy out the fee simple it may be made after the lease has expired. In addition, certain restrictions on the right to buy out the fee simple set out in s.16 of the Landlord and Tenant (Ground Rents) (No. 2) Act 1978 (which, among other things, preclude the right to acquire the fee simple where the lease forming the basis of the application is of commercial property or a building divided into a number of flats and contains certain rent review clauses) do not restrict the right to a reversionary lease.

Further statutory rights may be found in the Landlord and Tenant (Amendment) Act 1971 permitting the grant of sporting leases to sports club occupiers who satisfy certain requirements. There are also the rights, mentioned briefly above, to compensation for disturbance and improvements under Pt IV of the 1980 Act. In addition, the Housing (Private Rented Dwellings) Act 1982 confers statutory rights on a rapidly diminishing category of controlled tenants.

The above rights do not apply to residential tenancies falling within the scope of the Residential Tenancies Act 2004. Under s.192 of the Residential Tenancies Act 2004, a tenant may in exceptional cases be entitled to a new tenancy under Pt II of the 1980 Act, if, and only if, they have served a notice of intention to claim relief under that Act prior to September 1, 2009, being five years from the date of coming into effect of the 2004 Act.

Mortgages

I. TYPES OF MORTGAGES

Traditionally, a mortgage occurred where legal or equitable title to an interest in land was transferred by its owner (the mortgagor) as security for a loan, one of the conditions for the transfer being that if the loan was repaid on the due date, the borrower would get back title to the land. The transfer of land to the lender (the mortgagee) provided him with security for the loan and gave him priority over other creditors of the mortgagor.

Where the mortgage involved a transfer of legal ownership to the mortgagee, it was known as a legal mortgage.

LEGAL MORTGAGES AND CHARGES

The standard principle that a legal mortgage transfers legal ownership of the mortgaged property to the mortgagee has been amended by the Registration of Title Act 1964 (the "1964 Act") and the Land and Conveyancing Law Reform Act 2009 (the "2009 Act").

Under the 1964 Act, legal mortgages over registered land could only be created by registered charge. A registered chargee did not receive a transfer of ownership in the charged land although he or she had similar powers to a legal mortgagee in a number of respects.

Section 89 of the 2009 Act provided that, from December 1, 2009, legal mortgages of unregistered land could only be created by a charge by deed, known as a legal charge. Legal charges, like registered charges, are not "mortgages" in the strict sense of the word as they do not involve a transfer of ownership.

EQUITABLE MORTGAGES

Equitable mortgages involve a transfer of equitable title only, with legal title remaining in the mortgagor. They may arise in a number of different situations.

First, where there has been an agreement to create a legal mortgage but the necessary formalities for the creation of that mortgage at law (e.g. transfer of legal title to the mortgagee) have not been satisfied, a mortgage can nonetheless arise in equity.

Secondly, an equitable mortgage may arise where the interest being mortgaged is equitable in nature, e.g. the equity of redemption under a prior legal or other mortgage, or the interest of a beneficiary under a trust.

Thirdly, there can be an equitable mortgage by deposit of title deeds. Such mortgages differ from other legal and equitable mortgages insofar as they do not have to satisfy writing requirements. Traditionally, this form of mortgage was a popular one with Irish banks, but often created evidentiary problems for them at a later date when the customer alleged that the title deeds were lodged only for safekeeping.

The restrictions on the creation of mortgages contained in the 1964 Act and the 2009 Act apply only to legal mortgages and do not preclude in any way the creation of equitable mortgages over registered or unregistered land.

II. EQUITY'S INTERVENTION IN RELATION TO MORTGAGES

Equity has also intervened to protect the mortgagor under legal mortgages. The principles developed in this context apply by analogy to registered and legal charges.

EQUITABLE RIGHT TO REDEEM AT ANY TIME

First, equity intervened to protect the mortgagor's right to redeem. Originally, if the mortgagor did not repay on the date due, the mortgagee could keep the property forever. Out of sympathy for the mortgagor, who was often placed in an invidious position by the stronger bargaining power of the mortgagee, equity recognises that a mortgagor has a right to redeem at any time, even after the date for repayment had passed. Such a right cannot be taken away by clauses in the mortgage/charge (but may be lost if the property is lawfully sold by the mortgagee, in which case the equity of redemption (see below) will apply).

EQUITY OF REDEMPTION

In the event that the mortgaged or charged property is sold, equity also recognises the mortgagor as having a right to receive such monies (if any) left over out of the proceeds of the sale once the debt, interest and costs of sale have been discharged. This right, which is known as the equity of redemption, is an equitable interest belonging to the mortgagor which may itself be mortgaged by way of equitable mortgage as discussed above.

SCRUTINY OF TERMS IN MORTGAGES

As well as recognising the rights referred to above, equity also reserves the right to strike down clauses in mortgages on the basis that:

(a) They conflict with the equitable right to redeem referred to above;

(b) They are harsh and unconscionable.

Conflict with equitable right to redeem

The following provisions may be struck down on the basis that they unfairly restrict the mortgagor's right to redeem:

(a) Clauses which expressly state that there is no right to redeem. These clauses are always invalid.

(b) Clauses which confer an option to purchase on the mortgagee. These clauses are automatically void. If the mortgagee were to exercise this option, the mortgagor's right to redeem would be completely ineffective. Such clauses may, however, be upheld if they can be seen as being part of a different transaction from the mortgage.

(c) Clauses which postpone the right to redeem. Such clauses are valid, provided that:

  (i) They are not too harsh;

  (ii) They do not take away all value from the equity of redemption by making the right to redeem illusory, e.g. *Fairclough v Swan Brewery Co. Ltd* ([1912] A.C. 565).

(d) Collateral advantages. Collateral advantages are extra rights which are conferred on a mortgagee over and above his right to repayment of the money loaned. The right to claim interest on the loan would not be a collateral advantage since it constitutes an integral part of repayment. However, common examples of collateral advantages are to be seen in the tied-house agreements entered into between breweries and publicans, whereby the brewery lends the publican the money to buy the pub, and the publican covenants, as part of the mortgage agreement, only to sell beer from that particular brewery.

  Collateral advantages which persist after redemption are unenforceable since to uphold them would conflict with the equity of redemption, which says that on repayment of the loan and interest the mortgagor ought to regain ownership free from any restraints. This was laid down in the case of *Noakes & Co. Ltd v Rice* ([1902] A.C. 24) where a tied-house agreement which purported to persist after redemption was held unenforceable.

Noakes & Co. Ltd v Rice was applied in two subsequent cases: *Browne v Ryan* ([1901] 2 I.R. 653) and *Bradley v Carritt* ([1903] A.C. 253). In *Browne v Ryan*, the mortgagor agreed to sell the mortgaged land within 12 months through the mortgagee who was an auctioneer. The clause was designed to generate business for the mortgagee. Even if he redeemed the mortgage before the 12 months were up, he was still obliged to sell his land. For this reason, the clause was struck down as conflicting with the equity of redemption.

In *Bradley v Carritt* a number of shares in a tea company were mortgaged. One aim of the mortgage was to give the mortgagee, who was a tea broker, the controlling interest in the tea company. The mortgage provided that if the mortgagee did not get the brokerage for the sale of the company's tea, the mortgagor would pay him the amount of the commission that the mortgagee would have got as broker. Once again, this clause was held to be unenforceable because the collateral advantage persisted even after the mortgage was redeemed.

However, as with options to purchase, collateral advantages which persist after redemption may be permissible provided that they are contained in a separate transaction from the mortgage. This has always been the case in relation to options to purchase, but was established in relation to collateral advantages by the case of *Kreglinger v New Patagonia Meat and Cold* Storage Co. Ltd ([1914] A.C. 25). In that case it was held that a collateral advantage which persisted after redemption was enforceable even though it was granted at the same time and was contained in the same document as the mortgage. The House of Lords found nonetheless that the grant of a collateral advantage was a separate transaction from the mortgage.

Unduly harsh or unconscionable

Equity may strike down clauses in mortgage agreements on the ground that they are too harsh. It has been stated that a clause postponing the right to redeem may be struck down on the grounds of unconscionability. Another type of clause vulnerable to an unconscionability finding is the collateral advantage.

Originally, equity was very suspicious of collateral advantages. Money-lending legislation provided for a maximum rate of interest on loans. The device of collateral advantages was used to circumvent this and for this reason equity had a tendency to declare collateral advantages void. However, collateral advantages are now enforceable provided that they are not oppressive or unconscionable. In *Biggs v Hoddinott*, a collateral advantage combined with a postponement clause was held to be permissible.

Biggs v Hoddinott ([1898] 2 Ch. 307)

Facts: This was a tied-house agreement contained in a mortgage of a pub. It was agreed that the mortgage would not be redeemable for five years and, so long as the mortgage continued, the mortgagor could not sell any beer other than that of the mortgagee brewery.

Held: The agreement was permissible. Since it only postponed redemption for five years, it did not infringe the equity of redemption. In this case it was stated that there was no presumption that a collateral advantage was obtained by pressure, duress or undue influence. The person alleging unconscionability must bear the burden of proving it.

Unconscionability in this context means morally reprehensible dealing. The court takes into account the harshness of the collateral advantages for the mortgagor, the benefit they confer on the mortgagee and the relative bargaining strengths of both parties.

Cityland Property (Holdings) Ltd v Dabrah ([1968] Ch. 166)

Facts: A mortgagor had purchased a freehold estate from a landlord. Previously he had only been a lessee. The landlord said that the mortgagor could leave some of the purchase price unpaid provided that he gave the landlord a mortgage over the property. The mortgage had to be paid back in amounts which were much greater than the amount of the purchase price left unpaid.

Held: Given the parties' unequal bargaining power, the provisions regarding repayment of the mortgage could not be enforced. It is worth contrasting the decision in Cityland with that reached in the following case.

Multiservice Bookbinding Ltd v Marden ([1979] Ch. 84)

Facts: The mortgagor borrowed money in order to expand his business. However, at the same time, the mortgagee wanted to use the mortgage as an investment. It was provided that the amount repayable would be calculated by reference to the Swiss franc. However, the Swiss franc increased dramatically in value against the pound, so the mortgagor had a lot more to pay back. The mortgagor argued that this was unconscionable.

Held: The court rejected the mortgagor's argument, and upheld the clause, because he had got independent legal advice at the time of entering into the mortgage.

III. Rights of a Mortgagor

The mortgagor (this term is used in the broad sense to refer also to legal and registered chargors) has a number of rights, in particular the right to redeem the property. He has a legal right to redeem up to the date specified in the mortgage document and has, after that date, an equitable right to redeem. The right to redeem may be lost if the mortgagee gets a sale order from the court, or if the mortgagee exercises his statutory power of sale (see below). Normally the mortgagor must give reasonable notice of his intention to redeem or, alternatively, pay six months' interest. The purpose of this requirement is to give the mortgagee the opportunity to look elsewhere to find a replacement investment for his capital. The mortgagor must repay the principal sum, interest and the costs of the mortgagee. The mortgagee is entitled to all reasonable costs.

The mortgagor may make an inter vivos transfer of his equity of redemption to another party, but this party will usually take subject to the mortgage. He cannot sell the property free from the mortgage unless he redeems or gets the mortgagee to join in the conveyance.

IV. Rights of a Mortgagee

In this section, as in the 2009 Act, the term "mortgagee" is not confined to legal or equitable mortgagees in the strict sense, but also includes legal and registered chargees.

The three main rights with which a mortgagee is usually concerned is the right to possession, the right of sale and the right to appoint a receiver.

As far as these rights are concerned, a distinction has to be drawn between mortgagees holding under mortgages and charges, the creation of which pre-dates December 1, 2009, and those holding under charges and equitable mortgages created on or after that date.

V. Rights of a Mortgagee under a pre-2009 Act Mortgage

At the outset, it should be said that considerable uncertainty as to the rights of a pre-2009 Act mortgagee (which term is also used to refer to registered chargees under charges which pre-date the 2009 Act) has been created by the 2009 Act. The Act repeals pre-existing statutory provisions in relation to mortgagees' rights, without re-enacting any equivalent provisions applicable to pre-2009 Act mortgagees. Although it was originally thought that these pre-existing statutory provisions would continue, by reason of s.27 of the Interpretation Act 2005 (the "2005 Act"), to apply to pre-2009 Act mortgagees despite their repeal, some doubt has been cast on this by a recent decision of the High Court, discussed below.

THE RIGHT TO POSSESSION

A legal mortgagee under a legal mortgage, the creation of which pre-dates December 1, 2009, was traditionally entitled to possession as soon as the ink is dry on the mortgage. This has been established since the case of *Fourmaids Ltd v Dudley Marshall (Properties) Ltd* ([1957] Ch. 317) and is based on the transfer of legal title effected by a legal mortgage in the traditional sense. This right, not being statutory in nature, does not appear to have been affected by the 2009 Act and continues to subsist in respect of legal mortgages pre-dating the 2009 Act.

Registered charges, on the other hand, did not involve a transfer of ownership and the right of a registered chargee to possession was dealt with specifically by s.62(7) of the 1964 Act which provided that when repayment of the principal money secured by the instrument of charge had become due, the registered owner of the charge or his personal representative might apply to the court in a summary manner for possession of the land.

Section 62(7) (along with various other statutory provisions relating to pre-2009 Act mortgagees) was repealed by the 2009 Act without any replacement provision being introduced in respect of pre-2009 Act mortgages. It was thought that s.62(7) (along with other statutory rights of pre-2009 Act mortgagees) would continue in existence pursuant to s.27 of the 2005 Act which protects rights accrued as of the date of repeal. However, by its own terms the right of a registered chargee under s.62(7) only accrued when the principal monies fell due. Accordingly, whether or not a pre-2009 Act registered charge has a right to possession under s.62(7) would appear to depend on whether or not the principal monies under the registered charge were due as of November 30, 2009, this being the day prior to the repeal of s.62(7). This is the view taken by Dunne J. in the very recent decision of *Start Mortgages v Gunn* (unreported, High Court, July 29, 2011), a decision which has far-reaching implications not just for the purposes of s.62(7) but also for other statutory rights of mortgagees repealed by the 2009 Act.

Traditionally, equitable mortgagees were not entitled to automatic possession but could apply to court for an order granting them possession.

THE RIGHT OF SALE

There may be an express clause in the mortgage giving the mortgagee the power of sale. Mortgagees under mortgages created by deed had a statutory power of sale under s.19(1)(i) of the Conveyancing Act 1881 (the "1881 Act"). The power arose wherever the mortgage payments were overdue, but before it could become exercisable, required at least one of the following to be satisfied:

(i) A notice must have been served on the mortgagor requiring payment of the overdue money, followed by a failure on the part of the mortgagor to make payment within three months of the service of the notice; or
(ii) Interest under the mortgage must have been in arrears for two months; or
(iii) A covenant in the mortgage deed (other than a repayment covenant) must have been breached.

Sections 19 and 20 of the 1881 Act were among the statutory provisions repealed by the 2009 Act. It was thought that they would continue in existence in respect of pre-2009 Act mortgagees by reason of s.27 of the 2005 Act; however, this assumption can no longer be automatic following the decision of Dunne J. referred to above and it may be that amending legislation is necessary to enable pre-2009 Act mortgagees to continue to rely on the statutory power of sale, at least in circumstances where the mortgage payments were not overdue as of November 30, 2009. However, many mortgages contain an express power of sale which can be relied on as an alternative to the statutory power; this may mitigate any repeal of ss.19 and 20.

THE RIGHT TO APPOINT A RECEIVER

As regards pre-2009 Act mortgagees, the position in relation to the power to appoint a receiver mirrors that outlined above in relation to the power of sale. A mortgagee by deed traditionally had a statutory power to appoint a receiver under the 1881 Act, arising in the same circumstances as the statutory power of sale under the same Act outlined above. There might also be an express power in the mortgage. The effect of the repeal of the 1881 Act and the question of whether or not s.27 of the 2005 Act operates to preserve the statutory power in relation to pre-2009 Act mortgagees is, at present, unclear for the reasons stated above.

The mortgagor has a discretion as to whom he appoints as receiver. The appointment must be in writing. The receiver is the agent of the mortgagee and the mortgagee is liable for his defaults unless the mortgage deed provides otherwise. However, by appointing a receiver the mortgagee cannot be regarded as taking possession and so is not strictly liable to account.

MORTGAGES

VI. Rights of a Mortgagee under a post-2009 Act Mortgage

Sections 97–111 of the 2009 Act set out general principles regarding the statutory powers and rights of mortgagees holding under mortgages (which term is used by the 2009 Act to include registered and legal charges) created on or after December 1, 2009.

The right of possession

Section 97 governs the obtaining by a mortgagee of a court order for possession of the mortgaged property. Such an order must be sought if the mortgagee wants to take possession, unless the mortgagor consents in writing to such taking. The granting of the order is at the discretion of the court and may be made on such terms and conditions, if any, as the court thinks fit.

Section 98 entitles a mortgagee to seek an emergency order for possession in order to protect mortgaged property abandoned by the mortgagor. Such order may be applied for either in the District Court or in any court already seised of any applications or proceedings relating to the mortgaged property. There must be reasonable grounds for believing, first, that the property is abandoned and, secondly, that possession urgently needs to be obtained to prevent deterioration of or damage to the property or entry on it by trespassers or unauthorised persons. The making of the order is at the discretion of the court and may be made on such terms and conditions as the court sees fit. In particular, the court may specify the duration of the occupation and any works which should or may be carried out by the mortgagee, together with any costs and expenses to be added to the mortgage debt.

Section 99 provides that a mortgagee in possession of property (or, in the case of a receiver appointed by the mortgagee, a receiver) shall sell or lease the mortgaged property within a reasonable time. This may be varied by the terms of the court order granting possession.

Section 100(4) provides that an application for sale under s.100(3) may be heard together with an application for possession under s.97(2). Section 100(5) excludes the mortgagee from liability for any involuntary loss resulting from the sale and s.100(6) allows a mortgagee exercising the power of sale to recover all deeds and documents relating to the property to which a purchaser would be entitled.

Section 101(1) allows the court, when dealing with an application under s.97 or s.100, where it appears that the mortgagor is likely to be able to pay his arrears and interest within a reasonable period, to adjourn the proceedings or stay the enforcement of an order, or even suspend it, or merely postpone the date for delivery of possession of the mortgaged property for such periods as the court thinks reasonable. If an order is suspended it may be subsequently revived and s.101(2) provides that any adjournment, stay postponement or suspension may be made subject to such terms and conditions with regard to payment as the court thinks fit, with an entitlement on the part of the court to revoke or vary such terms pursuant to s.101(3).

THE RIGHT OF SALE

Section 100 of the 2009 Act re-enacts, with some important variations, the substance of the various provisions in the Conveyancing Acts 1881–1911 governing the mortgagee's statutory power of sale. As was the case under the Conveyancing Acts, s.100(1) provides that one of three conditions must be satisfied: failure to comply with a notice requiring payment of the mortgage debt within three months after it has been served; interest under the mortgage in arrears for two months; or some other breach of covenant other than the payment of rent. However, s.100(1) also imposes an additional requirement of a 28-day notice, which must be served on the mortgagor after one or more of the above conditions have been fulfilled.

Even after the service of such a notice, s.100(2) provides that the power of sale shall not be exercisable without a court order unless the mortgagor gives written consent to its exercise. Section 100(3) provides that such order for sale is to be at the discretion of the court and subject to such terms and conditions, if any, as the court thinks fit.

Section 102 re-enacts the provisions of s.19(1)(i) of the 1881 Act and s.4 of the Conveyancing Act 1911 conferring supplementary powers on a mortgagee exercising a power of sale including the power to sell the property subject to prior charges, either together or in lots, by public auction, tender or private contract and subject to such conditions in relation to title as the mortgagee may see fit.

THE RIGHT TO APPOINT A RECEIVER

Section 108 deals with the power to appoint a receiver and re-enacts the provisions in the 1881 Act. Section 108(1) details the circumstances in which this power of appointment may be exercised by the mortgagee. As with s.100(1), one of the following must be satisfied before a receiver can be appointed: failure to comply with a notice requiring payment of the mortgage debt within three months after it has been served; interest under the mortgage in arrears for two months; or some other breach of covenant other than the payment of rent. However, the 28-day notice requirement introduced by s.100(1) as a pre-requisite to the exercise of the power of sale does not apply to the power to appoint a receiver; nor does this power require a court order before it is exercisable. The appointment must, however, be made in writing.

MORTGAGES

VII. Judgment Mortgages

When one person is found by the court to owe money to another, the court may grant the creditor a judgment mortgage over the debtor's land. The creditor has the right to have the land sold and the proceeds used to discharge his debt.

Prior to the coming into effect of the 2009 Act, any creditor who wished to obtain a judgment mortgage had to follow the procedure laid down by the Judgment Mortgage (Ireland) Acts 1850–1858. He was required to file an affidavit in the court where the judgment was granted, containing details of the court, the title of the action and the date and amount of the judgment awarded against the defendant, and identifying the parties to the judgment and the land owned by the defendant to which the judgment mortgage was to attach. The filing of the affidavit transferred all of the land in question to the creditor and vested it in him subject to the debtor's right to redeem on paying the outstanding money. The creditor now had a judgment mortgage and he could enforce his rights under the mortgage by seeking a well-charging order and an order for the sale of the land.

The law in relation to judgment mortgages created after December 1, 2009 is now laid down in Pt 11 of the 2009 Act, which replaces with substantial modification the provisions of the Judgment Mortgage (Ireland) Acts 1850 and 1858.

Section 116 of the 2009 Act states that an application to register a judgment mortgage against a person's estate or interest in land may be made to the Property Registration Authority by any creditor who has obtained a judgment (defined by s.115 as any decree or order of any court of record) against that person. Such judgment mortgage shall be registered in the Registry of Deeds or Land Registry as appropriate. The term "creditor" is defined by s.115(a) as including a creditor's authorised agent or one of a number of creditors who have obtained the same judgment.

Section 116(3)(a) clarifies the uncertainty arising from s.4 of the 1850 Act by confirming that there is no requirement to re-register a judgment mortgage in order to maintain its validity. Section 116(3)(b) also confirms that the fact that a judgment debtor has obtained a stay of execution does not prevent the registration of a judgment mortgage against the land. It also confirms that a judgment mortgage may be registered against the interest of a beneficiary under a trust for sale, despite the fact that the interest of such a beneficiary has traditionally been regarded as personal property.

Section 117 deals with the effect of registration and states that such registration under s.116 operates to charge the judgment debtor's estate or interest in the land with the judgment debt and entitles the judgment mortgagee to apply to the court for an order under s.117 or s.31 of the 2009 Act.

Transfer of Land

Transfer of land may take place inter vivos or on death. An inter vivos transfer is a transfer of land from a living person, which takes place by a deed transferring the land to the new owner. In the case of registered land (land, title to which is registered in the Land Registry) the transfer is only complete when the transferee has been entered on the Land Register as the new owner of the land.

An inter vivos transfer may be a gift or a sale, depending on whether consideration has been given for the transfer. A transfer of land on death takes place under a will or, if no valid will exists, according to the rules of intestacy. This chapter concentrates on inter vivos transfers or, as they are referred to in relation to unregistered land, conveyances. The procedure for the transfer of land and other property on death is dealt with in Chapter 12: Succession Law.

In relation to any inter vivos transfer of either registered or unregistered land, it is vital to consider the Family Home Protection Act 1976. This Act applies where the present owner of the property is married, and the property to be sold is presently a family home. The failure of the non-owning spouse to give her written consent to the transfer may render it void. See below at III. The Family Home Protection Act 1976.

Previously, certain words of limitation ("in fee simple"/"and his/her heirs") had to be used in order for the fee simple estate in unregistered land to be transferred inter vivos. This has now been abolished both prospectively and retrospectively by s.67 of the Land and Conveyancing Law Reform Act 2009 (the "2009 Act"). Even prior to the coming into effect of the 2009 Act, words of limitation were not required when transferring registered land inter vivos. Transferring registered land is, in general, a simpler process than conveying unregistered land, although there still remain certain pitfalls for the purchaser.

Prior to a sale of land taking place it is important that the prospective purchaser find out what exactly he is buying. He needs to find out:

- whether the person selling has a fee simple estate; and
- whether there are any third party interests (easements, covenants, trusts, estoppels, etc.) burdening the land.

This process is known as investigation of title. The task of investigation of title differs as between registered and unregistered land. Most land in Ireland is registered land in the sense that details of its ownership are registered in the Land Registry. However, much land still remains unregistered.

I. INVESTIGATION OF TITLE TO UNREGISTERED LAND

DETERMINING WHETHER THE VENDOR HAS A FEE SIMPLE ESTATE

The transferee must make investigation of title to check that the transferor actually has the interest which he is purporting to transfer. In theory, it is necessary for the vendor to deduce title back for 15 years (the previous period of 40 years having been reduced to 15 years by s.56 of the 2009 Act). The vendor has first to show a good root of title which is at least 15 years old. A good root of title basically means a deed for value conveying the fee simple estate in the relevant land. In addition, the vendor will have to trace an unbroken chain of title from the root of title right up to the document giving him ownership of the land.

IDENTIFYING THIRD PARTY INTERESTS

Even when good title is shown, the purchaser needs to concern himself with the possibility of third parties having interests in the land. Examples of potential third party interests are as follows:

- Easements
- Profits à prendre
- Covenants
- Estoppel rights
- Rights under an express trust
- Rights under an implied trust

Looking at the above list, many easements and profits are legal interests. The others are equitable interests and therefore weaker in one respect. A purchaser of unregistered land is bound automatically by all legal third party interests. Normally he is bound by any equitable third party interests as well. However, he can take free of equitable third party interests, provided that he can show himself to be the purchaser of the legal estate without notice of these interests, which, additionally, have not been created by any document registered in the Registry of Deeds.

The purchaser of the legal estate without notice

As explained briefly in Ch.1, this individual is known as *equity's darling* because equity does not consider that he should be bound by equitable interests. In order to qualify as equity's darling a transferee must be a purchaser. An individual who receives property under a will or as a gift can never qualify.

Secondly, the transferee must have purchased the legal estate in the property. A transferee who merely obtains equitable ownership of the property by purchasing the interest of a beneficiary under a trust is bound by all other equitable interests attaching to the property.

Thirdly, and most importantly, the transferee must have no notice of the equitable interests. This means that he must have no actual or constructive knowledge of their existence. Even if the transferee did not actually know of the existence of the interests at the time he purchased the property, he may still be bound by them. A purchaser is regarded as having constructive notice of all interests which would have been evident to a purchaser taking reasonable care and making reasonable inquiries. The standard of care in this respect is quite high. A negligent purchaser can never be equity's darling.

Moreover, the concept of notice extends beyond actual or constructive knowledge in two respects. First, it includes the concept of imputed notice. A purchaser is held responsible for the actual or constructive knowledge of his solicitor. This is of particular concern to the purchaser, since a solicitor, being a professional in conveyancing transactions, has to keep to a very high standard of care in order to avoid being fixed with constructive knowledge.

In addition, the doctrine of notice incorporates the extremely significant rule in *Hunt v Luck* ([1902] 1 Ch. 428). This case laid down the principle that a purchaser is automatically regarded as having constructive notice of the rights of everyone living on the property at the time of the sale. The one exception is if the purchaser has actually asked the relevant occupiers about their rights and they have denied that they have any. In that circumstance he is held entitled to take them at their word.

All in all, it may be quite difficult for a purchaser to show that he has had no notice of equitable interests attaching to the land. Even if he does manage to surmount this hurdle, he still has to consider the possibility that the equitable interests may have been contained in a document which has been registered in the Registry of Deeds.

The Registry of Deeds

The Registry of Deeds system (which permits the registration, in the Registry of Deeds, of memorials of written documents relating to unregistered land) significantly modifies the doctrine of notice as regards interests created by such documents. Equitable interests created by a document registered in the

Registry of Deeds will normally bind all future owners of the land, even purchasers of the legal estate without notice, requiring prospective purchasers to make very careful searches in the Registry of Deeds.

The statute currently regulating the Registry of Deeds system is the Registration of Deeds and Titles Act 2006 (the "2006 Act"), which also contains provisions applicable to registered land. Both the Registry of Deeds and the Land Registry now come under the control and management of the Property Registration Authority, a body established by the 2006 Act.

If a purchaser of unregistered land omits to register a memorial of their conveyance in the Registry of Deeds, they risk losing priority to a bona fide purchaser without notice, or indeed to any person who subsequently acquires an interest in the land by written instrument, registration of which in the Registry of Deeds pre-dates registration of their deed; the Registry of Deeds system provides that priority, as between interests created by written instrument, depends on the respective dates of registration of the instruments and not the dates on which they were executed. The one exception is where the subsequent purchaser has actual notice of the prior unregistered deed at the date of registering their deed; in such cases, they are precluded from claiming the benefit of prior registration.

The consequences of the Registry of Deeds system is that the standard doctrine of notice outlined in the previous section is generally confined to equitable interests which, not being created by written instrument, are not capable of being registered in the Registry of Deeds, for example, interests under resulting or constructive trusts.

II. Investigation of Title to Registered Land

The introduction of registered land was designed to simplify conveyancing and to get rid of the many complications which ensue in the course of conveying unregistered land. The policy behind the registered land system was twofold: it aimed both to excuse the vendor from the duty of having to deduce title and to relieve the purchaser from the duty of having to investigate it.

The law applicable to registered land is to be found in the Registration of Title Act 1964 (the "1964 Act") (as amended by the 2006 Act and the 2009 Act), and the statutory instruments passed thereunder.

The thinking behind the introduction of a system of registered land was that prospective purchasers should merely have to check the Land Register in order to discover the interests which existed in relation to the land. If interests existed which were not referred to on the Register, the purchaser would not be bound by them. At this point the Registration of Title system appears to be a purchaser's Utopia. He merely has to consult the Register. However, the doctrine of overriding interests contained in s.72 of the 1964 Act represents the fly in the ointment so far as the purchaser of registered land is concerned. Such overriding interests do not have to be registered. They bind purchasers automatically, whether or not they are recorded on the Register. The list of interests in s.72(1) includes leases for 21 years or less, as well as squatters' rights, and certain easements. The most important overriding interest is contained in s.72(1)(j), namely, the rights of any person in actual occupation of the land at the time of the sale. There are a number of cases on the interpretation of this subsection, which need to be known in detail.

However, in one respect at least the registered land system makes investigation of title considerably easier. There is no longer a need for evidence of title deeds in order to identify whether the vendor has a fee simple estate. This can be ascertained merely by consulting the Register.

WHY IS SOME LAND REGISTERED LAND?

Much registered land was registered because its registration was made compulsory. There is provision under s.24 of the 1964 Act for a ministerial order to be made designating a particular county as a compulsory registration area. As of June 1, 2011, compulsory registration, introduced on a county-by-county basis over the period of 1970–2011, now applies to all counties in Ireland, including Dublin. Compulsory registration does not oblige all owners of unregistered land to register their title immediately; however, when the land in a compulsory registration area is conveyed to a purchaser, or demised by way of lease for more than 21 years, the purchaser/lessee must register in order to get a good title. Any owner of unregistered land can also apply at any time to be put on the Register voluntarily.

ADMINISTRATION OF THE REGISTRATION OF TITLE SYSTEM

The Registration of Title system is administered by the Land Registry. Both the Land Registry and the Registry of Deeds are now under the control of a body known as the Property Registration Authority.

There may be as many as three distinct Registers kept in relation to each piece of registered land:

(a) Register of ownership of freehold land.
(b) Register of ownership of leasehold interests (only leasehold interests with at least 21 years left to run may be registered on this register).
(c) Register of incorporeal hereditaments in gross. This does not apply to easements because they are not hereditaments in gross but includes profits and rentcharges.

Each Register is contained in a Folio, which is further divided into three parts. Part 1 contains a description of the land, making reference to the precise location of the land on the Land Registry Map. It sets out the boundaries of the land. Part 2 contains the name and address of the person or persons currently entitled to the freehold interest, leasehold interest or incorporeal hereditaments, depending on the particular Register. Part 3 lists any charges and mortgages over the land, along with any burdens which may be registered as registered burdens, e.g. easements or restrictive covenants.

CLASS OF TITLE HELD BY THE REGISTERED OWNER

Sometimes an occupier of land might seek to register their interest in land but the validity of their claim might be in doubt. There is provision to give them a non-absolute title until such time as they can prove their title conclusively.

The classes of title recorded on the Register are as follows:

(i) Absolute title.
(ii) Qualified title.
   If an applicant for registration has difficulty in proving title, he may be put into this latter class. The entry on the Register would contain a provision outlining the particular flaws in title. For example, in relation to a particular qualified title, a note might be entered stating that, as this title could only be shown since 1960, the title granted is subject to any rights arising before 1960.
(iii) Possessory title.
   This title may be granted to a squatter who has been in adverse possession of land for less than the 12-year limitation period. Once the squatter gets over the 12 years he can have a qualified title saying that he has rights against the dispossessed owner and all persons claiming through the dispossessed owner but not against persons claiming through another source. Title acquired under Irish Land Commission Grants (which did not investigate the tenant's title) was traditionally registered as possessory, but again could be upgraded after a number of years.
(iv) Good leasehold title.
   A good leasehold title gives a tenant a title to the leasehold interest in property, but it expressly states that it does not affect the right of any person which conflicts with the right of the lessor. This form of title would be used to designate a leasehold owner in a situation where the tenant's lease was valid but the landlord had some problem in showing his title to the land. The phrase "converting titles" refers to the practice of moving a title out of one class and into another, e.g.

raising a squatter's possessory title up to a qualified title after he has shown 12 years' adverse possession.

IDENTIFYING THIRD PARTY INTERESTS

Third party interests in registered land are divided into:

(a) Registrable burdens
(b) Overriding interests

(a) Registrable burdens

Registrable burdens are third party interests which are entitled to be recorded on the Register. If registered, they bind all transferees of the land. If these interests are unregistered, purchasers take free of them, but they still bind individuals who receive the land as a gift. The first thing that a purchaser of registered land ought to do is to check the Register to see which burdens are recorded on it.

A list of registrable burdens is provided in s.69(1) of the 1964 Act. The most important are as follows:

- A charge on the land created after first registration.
- A rentcharge or fee farm or other perpetual rent.
- A vendor's lien on the land for unpaid purchase money.
- A lease for more than 21 years (this must not only be registered as a burden on the freehold Register but also requires registration in its own right on the leasehold Register).
- A judgment or order of a court, e.g. property adjustment orders.
- A judgment mortgage.
- Any easement or profit created by express grant after first registration.
- Freehold covenants.
- Rights of residence.
- A power of distress or entry.

(b) Overriding interests

In contrast to registrable burdens, checking the Register will not provide a purchaser with immunity from overriding interests. As already stated, these are interests which bind the purchaser without the need for registration. They are listed in s.72(1) of the 1964 Act as follows:

- Any estate duty, farm tax, gift tax and inheritance tax.
- Any annuities or rentcharges under the Land Purchase Acts.
- All public rights of way.
- All customary rights.
- Certain easements and profits.
- Leases for 21 years or less.
- Rights acquired or in the course of being acquired under the Statute of Limitations 1957.
- The rights of every person in actual occupation of the land or in receipt of the rents and profits thereof save where inquiry is made of such person and the rights are not disclosed (s.72(1)(j)).

FURTHER DETAIL ON s.72(1)(j)

Rights

Section 72(1)(j)) only applies where the person in actual occupation has rights in relation to the land. *National Provincial Bank v Ainsworth* ([1965] A.C. 1175) stated that the word "rights" under the United Kingdom equivalent of s.72(1)(j) referred to proprietary rights and did not include personal rights such as rights under a licence or under the Family Home Protection Act 1976. *Ainsworth* was followed in Ireland by *Guckian v Brennan* ([1981] I.R. 478) in which it was held that a wife's rights under the Family Home Protection Act 1976 were personal rights only and could not constitute overriding interests. In *Webb v Pollmount Ltd* ([1966] Ch. 584) it was stated that an option to purchase land was a proprietary right and could constitute an overriding interest.

Actual occupation

The second condition for s.72(1)(j) is that the person who has the rights must be in actual occupation of the land at the time of the sale. There are a number of cases detailing what constitutes actual occupation. In *Williams & Glyns Bank v Boland* ([1981] A.C. 487) a wife had an interest in the family home under a constructive trust. She was living there with her husband. It was held that she was in actual occupation for the purposes of the subsection. A wife did not have to have sole possession to come under s.72(1)(j). Joint possession with her husband was sufficient.

In *Kingsnorth Finance v Tizard* ([1996] 1 W.L.R. 783) a wife invoked the United Kingdom equivalent of the subsection. She was sleeping elsewhere but came in every day to clean and care for the children. She had also left most of her belongings in the house. It was held that she too was in actual occupation. In *Wallcite Ltd v Ferrishurst Ltd* ([1999] 1 All E.R. 977) it was held that it is not necessary for the person in actual occupation to be in occupation of the whole of the land over which his interest subsists; it is sufficient if he is in actual occupation of a part of it at the time of the sale. This will cause the interest to bind the purchaser even in respect of the unoccupied part. The result of the decision is that an individual who wishes to purchase part of registered land should not only make inquiries about the rights of people living on the part he is actually purchasing, but should also inquire of all the individuals living on any part of the registered land whether they have rights which attach to the part he is purchasing.

In conclusion, purchasers of registered land are not bound by registrable burdens, which have not been registered. They are bound by overriding interests and by registered registrable burdens whether they have notice of them or not. The doctrine of notice does not apply to registered land. Individuals who receive registered land as a gift are bound by all third party interests over the land. The same position exists in relation to unregistered land.

RECTIFICATION OF THE REGISTER

Section 32 of the 1964 Act provides for rectification of errors on the Register. The Registrar may rectify the error, but he must first obtain the consent of the registered owner. If he fails to get this consent, he may apply to court for an order allowing rectification. The court will grant this order if it feels that such rectification may be carried out without injustice.

III. THE FAMILY HOME PROTECTION ACT 1976

The Family Home Protection Act 1976 (the "1976 Act") states that the family home cannot be conveyed by a spouse without the consent of the other spouse. The consent of the non-owning spouse is required in all cases, even when that spouse owns no interest at all, legal or equitable, in the family home.

If the consent is not obtained, the transfer is at risk of being void, unless it is to a *purchaser for full value*. A purchaser for full value is defined by the 1976 Act as a person who in good faith purchases an interest in property. The burden of proof is on the purchaser to show that this term applies to him.

The 1976 Act only applies to married couples and not to couples who are living together, but Pt 4 of the Civil Partnership and Certain Rights and Obligations of Cohabitants Act 2010 (the "2010 Act") discussed at Section IV below contains very similar provisions to the 1976 Act in relation to civil partners.

Whenever the student or practitioner is faced with a situation involving a mortgage, lease or sale of land, it is necessary to consider, first, whether this land is a family home. If it is, it is important to know whether the written consent of the vendor's spouse/civil partner has been obtained to the transfer.

i) DEFINITIONS IN THE FAMILY HOME PROTECTION ACT 1976

Conveyance

A conveyance is defined as including a mortgage, lease, and any disposition of an interest in property other than by will. It includes a contract to create any of the above. Case law has established that a transfer by operation of law, such as a judgment mortgage or possibly an estoppel, would not require spousal consent.

Family home

This is defined as a dwelling where the non-owning spouse ordinarily resides or has so resided before leaving the other spouse. Any building occupied as a separate dwelling constitutes a family home. The definition (as amended by s.54(1)(a) of the Family Law Act 1995 (the "1995 Act")) also includes all land usually occupied with the dwelling, being land that is subsidiary and ancillary to it, is required for amenity or convenience and is not being used or developed primarily for commercial purposes.

A house on a farm may be a family home, but the farmland itself would not be covered by the definition. It appears that if the conveyance is one which transfers both the farm and the house, it may be severed by the court so as to be void in so far as it relates to the house and valid in so far as it relates to the other property. A mobile home may constitute a dwelling.

Prior consent in writing

The consent must be in writing and executed before the conveyance takes place. However, the courts have been flexible in interpreting this requirement. In *Bank of Ireland v Hanrahan* (unreported, High Court, O'Hanlon J., February 10, 1987) the consent was given two hours after an equitable mortgage had been completed by the husband handing over the title deeds to the bank. The court held that there was an implied condition in the transfer of the title deeds that the bank would merely hold them for safekeeping and not for security for the loan until the wife's consent was completed.

Section 54(1)(b) of the 1995 Act amends the 1976 Act to provide that a spouse may make a general and open-ended consent in writing to future transfers of the family home. Once they sign such a document their consent to future transfers will no longer be necessary.

However, any consent under the 1976 Act, as amended, must be voluntary. It cannot be obtained by undue influence, duress, misrepresentation or mistake. It must be an informed consent. The spouse must appreciate the consequences of what she is signing. This has been demonstrated by *Bank of Ireland v Smyth* ([1993] 2 I.R. 102) and *Allied Irish Banks v Finnegan* ([1996] 1 I.L.R.M. 401) (discussed below). Courts will be particularly vigilant to ensure that a general consent under the 1995 Act is a fully informed consent.

ii) EXCEPTIONS TO THE REQUIREMENT OF CONSENT

Sale by co-owning spouses

Where the spouses are co-owners and parties to the sale, consent is not required from either of them. This was established by the case of *Nestor v Murphy* ([1979] I.R. 326) in which it was held that the purpose of the Act did not require consent in such cases. Obviously, both spouses had consented to the sale in that situation, even though they might not have complied with the formal requirements of the Act regarding consent.

Consent to contract of sale

Where a spouse has made an informed consent in writing to a contract of sale, there is no need for her to make a further, separate consent to the conveyance carrying out that contract.

Conveyance to the non-owning spouse

There is no need for a spouse to consent to a conveyance which is in her favour.

Conveyance subject to an agreement entered into with a third party before marriage

Because the obligation to convey was entered into before marriage, there is no need for the other spouse to consent.

Conveyances to a purchaser for full value

This is the most important exception. The 1976 Act states that a conveyance will not be void if it was made in favour of a purchaser for full value and defines a purchaser as someone who in good faith acquires an interest in property. *Somers v Weir* ([1979] I.R. 94) held that this provision incorporated the equitable doctrine of notice into the 1976 Act. A purchaser cannot be a purchaser in good faith if he has actual, constructive or imputed notice of the fact that consent ought to have been and/or has not been obtained (see above for an outline of the concept of notice).

In *Bank of Ireland v Smyth* ([1993] 2 I.R. 102) a purchaser was held to be fixed with constructive notice of the fact that a spouse's consent was invalid. The reason for the consent being invalid was that the spouse did not fully appreciate the implications of the document she was signing. It was held that the bank had constructive notice of the fact that the consent was invalid. Had they acted as a reasonable purchaser would have done they would have made inquiries into the wife's understanding of the transaction and discovered that she was not fully informed.

In *Allied Irish Banks plc. v Finnegan* ([1996] 1 I.L.R.M. 401) it was held that the onus of disproving actual or constructive knowledge lay on the individual or institution seeking to avail of the purchaser for value exception. This is a heavy burden to fulfil, given the known difficulties which attach to proving a negative fact.

Situations where consent can be dispensed with

Section 4 of the 1976 Act makes provision for dispensing with a spouse's consent:

* where the non-disposing spouse has deserted;
* where there is unsoundness of mind or mental disability on the part of the non-disposing spouse;
* where the non-disposing spouse cannot be found;
* where it is unreasonable for a spouse to withhold consent.

Hamilton v Hamilton ([1982] I.R. 466) establishes guidelines for deciding whether a refusal to consent is unreasonable. The court may take into account the relative financial positions of the parties, in addition to any emotional disturbance which may be caused to the spouse and/or the children by the trauma of having to leave the family home. It was emphasised that it is important to take both parties' points of view into account when deciding the question of reasonableness.

iii) Effect of conveyance in breach of the Family Home Protection Act 1976

Section 3(1) of the 1976 Act provides that where a spouse, without the prior written consent in writing of the other spouse, purports to convey any interest in the family home to any person except the other spouse, then the purported conveyance shall be void.

Section 54(1)(b) of the 1995 Act amends s.3(1) to provide that proceedings to have a conveyance declared void by reason of this section shall not be initiated after the expiration of six years from the date of the conveyance. It goes on to state that a conveyance shall be deemed not to be and never to have been void by reason of s.3(1) unless:

(i) it has been so declared by a court in legal proceedings instituted by a spouse prior to the expiration of six years from the date of the conveyance or the parties to the conveyance; or
(ii) the relevant spouses or their successors in title have so stated in writing before the expiration of this period.

There is provision for the extension of the six-year period in the case of a spouse who has been in actual occupation of the land concerned from immediately before the expiration of six years from the date of the conveyance concerned until the institution of the proceedings.

IV. THE CIVIL PARTNERSHIP AND CERTAIN RIGHTS AND OBLIGATIONS OF COHABITANTS ACT 2010

Part 4 of the 2010 Act contains provisions closely mirroring those in the 1976 Act (as amended by s.54 of the 1995 Act).

Under s.29, a civil partner may not convey an interest in the shared home without the prior written consent of the other civil partner. If he or she conveys without consent, proceedings may be instituted to have the conveyance deemed void before the expiration of six years from the date of the conveyance. This limitation period does not apply where the applicant is a civil partner who was in actual occupation of the shared home during the whole period from the date of the conveyance until immediately before the institution of the proceedings.

The exceptions to the requirement of consent are similar to those set out in the 1976 Act and the 2010 Act also incorporates the provision in s.54 of the 1995 Act to the effect that a general consent in writing of a civil partner to any future conveyance of any interest in the shared home is sufficient to constitute the necessary consent in writing.

11 Adverse Possession

The doctrine of adverse possession represents a way in which an individual can gain de facto rights through long user of someone else's land.

The Statute of Limitations 1957 (the "1957 Act") prevents tort actions being brought after a certain period of time. It also operates to prevent actions relating to land being brought after a certain period of time (usually 12 years but, as stated below, a longer period may apply in respect of land owned by State Authorities). If someone else has been in adverse possession of your land for that period, then your right to sue them and your consequent right to the land is extinguished. This gives that individual de facto rights and, so long as they remain in possession, their possession gives them a better title to the property than anybody else.

The policy factors in favour of extinguishment of title by adverse possession are as follows: the doctrine encourages speedy recourse to legal actions, the quieting of title and the economic use of land. It avoids the problems attracted by unadministered estates.

The doctrine of adverse possession was first introduced in the Real Property Limitation Act 1833 and is now contained in the 1957 Act. The relevant statutory provisions in the 1957 Act are as follows. Section 13(2) of the 1957 Act provides that no action to recover land shall be brought by any person, other than a State Authority, "after the expiration of twelve years from the date on which the right of action accrued to the person bringing it". Section 24 further provides that, at the expiration of the period fixed for a person to bring an action to recover land, the title of that person to the land shall be extinguished.

The 12-year period referred to in s.13(2) is expressly stated not to apply to a State Authority. Instead, s.13(1) of the 1957 Act makes it clear that State Authorities have 30 years to recover possession of land owned by them. The one exception is in the case of foreshore, where an even longer period applies. An action by a State Authority to recover foreshore may be brought at any time up to 60 years following the date on which the right of action accrued. In the case of land which is no longer foreshore, but which was foreshore at the date on which the right of action accrued, the period is either the 60-year period specified above, or 40 years from the date on which the land ceased to be foreshore, whichever is the lesser.

The following bodies fall within the definition of State Authority for the purposes of the 1957 Act: a Minister of State, the Commissioners of Public Works in Ireland, the Irish Land Commission, the Revenue Commissioners, the Attorney General and various North-South bodies listed in the British-Irish Agreement Act 1999. A local authority is not a State Authority for this purpose and is subject to the shorter period of 12 years.

Section 18(1) of the 1957 Act states that no right of action to recover land shall be deemed to accrue unless the land is in the possession (in this section referred to as adverse possession) of some person in whose favour the period of limitation can run. It further states that where, under the foregoing provisions of the 1957 Act, a right of action to recover land is statutorily deemed to accrue on a certain date, and no person is in adverse possession of the land on that date, the right of action shall not be deemed to accrue unless and until adverse possession is taken of the land.

The consequence of s.18(1) is that the mere fact that a person has been carrying out acts of trespass on land for more than 12 years (so as to give its owner a right of action against them) does not necessarily mean that the owner's title to the land is extinguished. Before this can occur, it is necessary to show that the trespasser's acts of trespass throughout a 12-year period are such as to amount to adverse possession. Most acts of trespass do not satisfy this requirement.

I. REQUIREMENTS FOR ADVERSE POSSESSION

The term "adverse possession" is not specifically defined in the 1957 Act. However, there are a number of judicial definitions of this term, in particular, that of the Supreme Court in *Murphy v Murphy* ([1980] I.R. 183) which states at 202 that:

> "In section 18 of the Act of 1957 adverse possession means possession of land which is inconsistent with the title of the true owner: this inconsistency necessarily involves an intention to exclude the true owner, and all other persons, from enjoyment of the estate or interest which is being acquired. Adverse possession requires that there should be a person in possession in whose favour time can run. Thus it cannot run in favour of a licensee or a person in possession as a servant or caretaker or a beneficiary under a trust ...".

This definition of adverse possession needs to be read in the light of s.14(1) of the 1957 Act which states that where the person bringing an action to recover land, or some person through whom he claims, has been in possession thereof and has while entitled thereto been dispossessed or discontinued his possession, the right of action shall be deemed to have accrued on the date of the dispossession or discontinuance. It would appear from this that dispossession/discontinuance is an additional component to adverse possession. However, the most recent case law generally treats dispossession/discontinuance as an essential requirement of adverse possession in any case.

Four conditions must be satisfied in order for adverse possession to occur. If s.18(1) is to be satisfied, all of these requirements must be present, not just at intervals throughout the 12-year period, but on a continuous basis throughout that period.

1. The person whose title is alleged to be extinguished must not have been in possession of the land during the relevant period.
2. Another person (a squatter) must have been in possession of the land throughout that period.
3. The squatter must have been in possession as a trespasser, without the permission of the owner.
4. The squatter must have had what is known as an *animus possidendi*.
5. Previously it was thought that there was a fifth requirement, namely that the squatter frustrate the purpose of the rightful owner. However, courts appear to be moving away from this.

i) THE PERSON WHOSE TITLE IS ALLEGED TO HAVE BEEN EXTINGUISHED MUST NOT HAVE BEEN IN POSSESSION OF THE LAND DURING THE RELEVANT PERIOD

Case law on adverse possession makes clear that the rightful owner must also have been dispossessed, or have discontinued possession, and that this dispossession or discontinuance must have lasted throughout the 12-year period relied on. Obviously, a person must first have a right to possession of land before he can be dispossessed. This is another reason why time does not run against landlords or persons with future interests.

Even slight acts of ownership by the rightful owner over the land during the 12-year period will negate dispossession. The acts do not have to be such that, if carried out by a squatter, they would constitute possession.

In *Browne v Fahy* (unreported, High Court, Kenny J., October 24, 1975), the fact that one of the owners walked over the land on a number of occasions was held to defeat adverse possession. In *Mulhern v Brady* ([2001] IEHC 23), the paper owner visited the property several times a year; requested a tenant of the adverse possessor to remove his cattle; advertised for planning permissions on numerous occasions; and also erected a "For Sale" sign on the property. It was held that the paper owner had exercised sufficient acts of ownership and maintained a continuing interest and connection with the land to warrant a defeat of any adverse possession claim. In the recent decision of *Moley v Fee* ([2007] IEHC 143), Laffoy J. held that the fact that the rightful owner brought an auctioneer to see the disputed plot some time in the late 1990s in the context of discussions for a sale to a third party, negated any allegation of dispossession.

The decision of *Feehan v Leamy* ([2000] IEHC 118) illustrates the difficulties of proving dispossession. In that case Finnegan J. held that there had been no discontinuance of possession, even though the only use to which the rightful owner had put the land was to visit it on a number of occasions each year when he would park his car and, standing on the road or in the gateway, look over the hedge or gate into the same. He stated that:

> "Insofar as the plaintiff's title is concerned the presumption is that it extends to the centre of the road and so when standing at the gate looking into the lands the plaintiff was in fact standing on his own lands … the plaintiff was exercising all the rights of ownership which he wished to exercise in respect of the lands pending the determination of litigation. I find as a matter of fact that he was not dispossessed."

This finding is controversial and contrasts with the concept of possession in the English case of *J.A. Pye (Oxford) Limited* ([2002] UKHL 30). In that case, although agents of the dispossessed owner had attended at the lands, they had not entered on the lands and their presence in the vicinity or at the entranceway did not amount to possession as far as the House of Lords was concerned.

Another controversial decision is *Dundalk UDC v Conway* (unreported, High Court, Blayney J., December 15, 1987). Here an area of land sloped down to a river. This area was only used by its owner when it was necessary to repair a bridge over the river. It was held that just because the owner had not gone near the land for 12 years and had not objected to his neighbour grazing cattle on, it did not mean he had gone out of possession. Insofar as this case indicates that failure to exercise rights over the land does not amount to dispossession/discontinuance if the rightful owner has no reason to exercise these rights during the relevant period, it would not appear to correspond with the established case law on this issue and indeed goes further than *Feehan v Leamy*, criticised above. It is perhaps best explained as an example of the rule in *Leigh v Jack*, discussed below, the continued relevance of which is now in question.

ii) Someone else (a squatter) has been in possession of the land

Such a person is usually known as a "squatter". In order for someone to qualify as a squatter, his acts over the land in question must amount to acts of possession. Merely playing on the land, keeping ponies there, walking and shooting are not normally equivalent to acts of possession.

There are a number of general judicial comments in relation to this requirement. Slade L.J. in *Powell v McFarlane* ([1979] 38 P. & C.R. 452) at 470 stated that:

> "If the law is to attribute possession of land to a person who can establish no paper title to possession, he must be shown to have both factual possession and the requisite intention to possess ('animus possidendi') … Factual possession signifies an appropriate degree of physical control. It must be a single and conclusive possession, though there can be a single possession exercised by or on behalf of several persons jointly. Thus an owner of land and a person intruding on that land cannot both be in possession of the land at the same time. The question what Acts constitute a sufficient degree of exclusive physical control must depend on the circumstances, in particular the nature of the land and the manner in which land of that nature is commonly used or enjoyed."

Lord O'Hagan in *The Lord Advocate v Lord Lovat* ((1880) 5 App. Cas. 273) emphasised that:

> "As to possession, it must be considered in every case with reference to the peculiar circumstances. The acts, implying possession in one case, may be wholly inadequate to prove it in another. The character and value of the property, the suitable and natural mode of using it, the course of conduct which the proprietor might reasonably be expected to follow with a due regard to his own interests—all these things, greatly varying as they must, under various conditions, are to be taken into account in determining the sufficiency of a possession."

In *Doyle v O'Neill* (unreported, High Court, O'Hanlon J., January 13, 1995) O'Hanlon J. stated:

> "In order to defeat the title of the original landowner, I am of opinion that the adverse user must be of a definite and positive character and such as could leave no doubt in the mind of a landowner alerted to his rights

that occupation adverse to his title was taking place. This is particularly the case when the parcel of land involved is for the time being worthless or valueless for the purposes of the original owner."

Clarke J. in the very recent case of *Dunne v Iarnród Éireann* ([2007] IEHC 314) emphasised that, for the purposes of adverse possession:

"[T]he nature of the possession which must be established is one which must be objectively viewed by reference to the lands concerned and the type of use which one might reasonably expect a typical owner to put those lands to."

A similar view was taken by Laffoy J. in the recent case of *Tracey Enterprises MacAdam Limited v Drury* ([2006] IEHC 381), in which she stated that:

"[T]he evidence does not establish that in the period from 1983 to 2000 the defendant's use of the disputed plot constituted possession. Apart from clearing waste from the disputed plot in a manner akin to abating a nuisance, the defendant's use was limited to sporadic incursions for the purpose of testing machinery following repair or service in the adjoining workshop. This is borne out by the defendant's reference in the letter of 17th November, 1993 to the fact that in the past, in common with others, he had used the disputed plot 'on occasion'. Having regard to the nature of the disputed plot, the manner in which it was used by the defendant between 1983 and 2000, which covers most of the crucial period between 1993 and 2005, would not have sent out a signal that the defendant was occupying the disputed plot to the exclusion of the true owner and all others."

By contrast, in *Griffin v Bleithin* ([1999] 2 I.L.R.M. 182), rather equivocal and intermittent acts over the course of the limitation period were held to amount to adverse possession. The premises consisted of a large garage, a shed and a yard. The one-time tenant failed to vacate the yard and shed following a notice to quit in 1974. After separating from his wife, he lived on the premises in a vehicle for a time. He was absent from the premises for prolonged periods owing to work commitments. By autumn of 1983, he had been absent from the yard for such a time that it was considered derelict. However, he was still held to have been in possession of the yard and shed (but not the large garage) for the requisite period due to the presence of his property in same.

If the squatter's user of land is on a non-exclusive basis only (i.e. it is shared with third parties unconnected to him and on the land without his permission), then it appears that it will not constitute possession for this purpose. In *Dunne* there was evidence that local children had kept ponies and horses on the lands used by the squatter during the period in respect of which he was alleging adverse possession. Clarke J. held that possession had not been shown, stating that:

> "[W]hile Mr. Dunne may well have been the predominant user of the lands at all material times I am not satisfied that he was the exclusive user (that is to say that he had excluded the local children entirely) until the late 1990's."

However, if the third parties had been on the land with the permission of the squatter (e.g. as his tenants or licensees) then he would be able to claim the benefit of their possession. In addition, it would be possible, if two persons had deliberately decided to share possession of land, that they could claim joint possession and in this way acquire a possessory title as co-owners.

Clarke J. in *Dunne* also distinguished between acts of possession and acts which were equally explicable as relating to the purported exercise of lesser rights, such as easements. In that case, grazing of the land had taken place on a consistent basis. However, Clarke J. stated that:

> "While I accept Mr. Dunne's evidence that in recent years more significant numbers of horses may have been present, I am not satisfied (having regard to all the evidence and, in particular the aerial photographs) that anything more than a small number (perhaps two or at most, on occasion, four) were present in the period up 1993. Such a number of animals being present is, in my view, at least as consistent with the exercise of grazing rights as with ownership in particular where no significant buildings have been constructed or are in use ... I am, therefore, satisfied that, where the extent of use of lands in respect of which adverse possession is claimed are consistent equally with establishing an easement or profit-à-prendre as with full ownership, then it is appropriate to infer the lesser rather than the greater entitlement."

It is possible that such equivocal acts, may, if continued for the requisite prescriptive period, result in the acquisition of an easement. However, they will not, in the absence of further evidence, give title by adverse possession.

One matter which can change relatively equivocal user into unequivocal exclusive possession is the erection of a fence or some other barrier by the squatter so as to exclude other persons from the land. In *Dunne*, Clarke J. regarded fencing as significant, but did not feel that it had been present for the requisite 12-year period, stating that:

> "I accept Mr. Dunne's evidence that he engaged from time to time in putting up some fencing but I am not satisfied that significant work was done in that regard prior to 1993. If Mr. Dunne had maintained a strict attitude to building and maintaining significant fencing, then it seems unlikely that the informal pathways to which I have referred could have been in existence. The fact that those pathways seem largely to disappear during the latter 1990s (from the evidence of the same aerial photographs) suggests that significant fencing only occurred at or around that time rather than earlier."

Battelle v Pinemeadow ([2002] IEHC 120) is an example of a case in which the erection of fencing was crucial to a finding of possession. Finnegan J., in this case, stated as follows:

> "[T]he first named Plaintiff set about cleaning up the area to the rear of his garden and incorporating it into his garden. He cleared away the briars and fenced the area completing this in the early 1980s. He erected a two metre high fence along the northern and southern boundaries and a five foot high fence at the top of the bank along by the river. He planted hundreds of plants and shrubs and completed three walkways inside the fenced area. He laid on electricity and installed garden lighting. He laid out garden furniture. In the mid 1980s he completed a water feature in granite comprising a waterfall and pond. All this was completed by the mid 1980s. On the evidence of the first named Plaintiff I am satisfied that the Plaintiffs had sole and exclusive possession of the plot incorporated by them into their garden from at the latest 1st January 1985 onwards."

This fits in with the definition of possession given in *Doyle v O'Neill*, namely, acts carried out by the squatter which are such as to leave no doubt in the mind of the rightful owner that occupation adverse to his title has taken place. Fencing is also a way in which the additional requirement of *animus possidendi*, discussed below, may be shown, and it may be seen from the judgments discussed above that the concepts of possession and *animus possidendi* are very closely linked.

iii) THE SQUATTER MUST HAVE BEEN IN POSSESSION WITHOUT THE PERMISSION OF THE RIGHTFUL OWNER

A person in possession with the permission of the owner cannot be regarded as being in adverse possession. This effectively means that tenants cannot be in adverse possession of the property the subject of their tenancy until (at the very least) their tenancy comes to an end. Tenants who stay on after the expiration of their tenancy without the permission of the landlord are regarded as adverse possessors for this purpose (although known as tenants at sufferance). Tenants who stay on with the permission of the landlord but without paying rent are known as tenants at will and become adverse possessors one year after the expiration of their tenancy (s.17(1) of the 1957 Act), unless the permission is renewed at that point. Where rent is accepted from tenants following the expiration of their lease or tenancy, they become a periodic tenant and will not be in adverse possession while that periodic tenancy subsists. However, it should be noted, as stated above, that non-payment of rent causes an oral periodic tenancy (though not a written periodic tenancy or a fixed-term lease) to cease to subsist.

As regards persons who, although not tenants, are in occupation of the land with the permission of the owner, such persons are effectively licensees and cannot be in adverse possession for the duration of their licence. However, licences, being personal rights only, come to an end on the death of either one of the parties thereto and one particular category of licence, the tenancy at will, determines early pursuant to s.17(1) as discussed above. Following the determination of the licence, permission ceases and (assuming the other requirements are satisfied) adverse possession commences. In addition, if a licence is qualified in nature, e.g. a licence to do certain things only, and the licensee exceeds that permission then they may be regarded as being in adverse possession. If a person is in possession of lands with the consent or licence of the owner, then his possession is not adverse: see *Hughes v Griffin* ([1969] 1 W.L.R. 1295).

Normally (in the absence of the payment and acceptance of rent, which would give rise to a periodic tenancy by implication) permission would have to be express in nature. However, on occasion, a licence could be implied from the conduct of the parties. An implied licence is more likely to be held present where the relationship is a family one than when no family ties exist. In *A v C* ([2007] IEHC 120), Laffoy J. refused a claim for adverse possession as between father and son on the basis of such an implied licence, stating that:

> "[O]n the evidence the occupation of the house and the use of the land were with the permission of the Testator. In their written submissions counsel for the defendants have listed a variety of factors which they

contend illustrate that the actuality of the occupation and use by the plaintiffs of the property of which they claim they were in adverse possession is inconsistent with the concept of adverse possession: that A continued to draw wages from the farming enterprise until 1992; that the materials used for the initial repairs of Blackacre House in 1983 and 1984 were funded by the Testator; that a site for a house for A was provided at Brownacre when that property was acquired; that A believed that Brownacre was to be his; that the permission of the Testator and the executors were sought for the construction of the wall in the yard; and the sharing of resources and machinery and the shared use of the yard. Counsel for the defendants submitted that the evidence established that A had the express permission of the Testator to use the house and farm. I have no doubt, taking an overview of the evidence, that the plaintiffs' use and occupation of the part of Blackacre House which they have occupied over the years since 1983 and A's use of the 30 acres of farmland was with the permission of the Testator. Moreover, I have no doubt that, whether the permission was actually expressed by the Testator in terms that, the occupation and use could continue for as long as the Testator wished, that was what A understood to be the position."

However, Finnegan J. refused to hold permission to have been present in *Battelle v Pinemeadow*. In that case the plaintiff had approached Cranford Limited, the rightful owner of the land, seeking permission to extend their garden, and had received a response from Cranford to the effect that it could not say whether it owned the land, and expressed a lack of interest in it. It was held that a licence would not be implied where the rightful owner, unclear as to its title, simply failed to make any objection to the occupier's use of the land.

iv) THE SQUATTER MUST HAVE HAD *ANIMUS POSSIDENDI*

There must have been an *animus possidendi* on the part of the squatter, i.e. an intention to possess the land to the exclusion of all others, even the true owner.

In *Murphy v Murphy* ([1980] I.R. 183), a testator's widow had an entitlement to portion of his land pursuant to a residue clause in his will. She was not aware of this and treated the land as vested in her two sons. After the younger son sold his share, the latter worked the land. The mother's title was held to have been extinguished by adverse possession on the part of the son.

This requirement was considered in detail by Black J. in *Convey v Regan* ([1952] I.R. 56) where he stated that:

"The basis of the principle seems to be that when a trespasser seeks to oust the true owner by proving acts of unauthorised and long continued user of the owner's lands, he must show that those acts were done with animus possidendi, and he must show this unequivocally. It is not, in my view, enough that, the acts may have been done with the intention of asserting a claim to the soil, if they may equally have been done merely in the assertion of a right to an easement or a profit-à-prendre. When the acts are equivocal – when they may have been done equally with either intention – who should get the benefit of doubt, the rightful owner or the trespasser? I think it should be given to the rightful owner."

In *Feehan v Leamy* ([2000] IEHC 118), Finnegan J. defined *animus possidendi* as "an intention to preclude the true owner and all other persons from enjoyment of the estate or interest which is being acquired". In that case, when gardaí were called to the lands in issue, the squatter informed them that the lands belonged to a man in America. According to Finnegan J., this failure by the squatter to assert ownership of the land negated *animus possidendi*.

An oral acknowledgment of the owner's title, even if not sufficient to bring the defence of acknowledgment into play, may serve to negate *animus possidendi*.

In *Tracey Enterprises MacAdam Limited v Drury* ([2006] IEHC 381), Laffoy J. stated that:

"[T]he evidence strongly suggests that prior to 2000 the plaintiff did not have the necessary animus possidendi to justify an inference that the possession was adverse. The defendant was not asserting a right of exclusive possession to the disputed plot. His justification for erecting the fences he erected at that time was to keep Mr. Quinn's straying cattle off land which he still regarded as commonage and away from the property he owned. After the solicitors acting for Dundrum formally objected to the erection of the fences by the defendant in September, 2001, the correspondence which passed between the solicitors indicates that on both sides the issue between the parties was seen as a paper title boundary dispute. It seems to me to be of particular significance that the plaintiff was not even at that stage asserting that he had established a possessory title to the disputed plot. The first time such assertion was made on his behalf was in 2004. Accordingly, I reject the defendant's assertion that he has acquired title by adverse possession to the disputed plot".

It is clear from the above dictum, which defines *animus possidendi* as "an assertion of exclusive possession", that the erection of fences by a squatter, with the intention of excluding the owner, may constitute adverse possession. However, if there is evidence that the fences were erected for some other reason, e.g. to prevent cattle straying, this will not constitute *animus possidendi.*

Griffin v Bleithin ([1999] 2 I.L.R.M. 182) demonstrates a liberal approach to the issue of *animus possidendi.* It was argued that the acts of the defendant were insufficient to show an *animus possidendi* on the ground that the defendant had been absent from the yard and shed for significant periods, and also that the acts of user by the defendant, such as using the yard for parking vehicles and the shed for storing materials, might have been merely intended to assert an easement rather than a right to possession. These arguments were rejected by Quirke J.

v) SQUATTER MUST FRUSTRATE PURPOSE OF RIGHTFUL OWNER

The statement of O'Hanlon J. in *Doyle v O'Neill*, that "the adverse user must be of a definite and positive character and such as could leave no doubt in the mind of a landowner alert to his rights that occupation adverse to his title was taking place" is also relevant in ascertaining *animus possidendi.*

The genesis of this possible fifth requirement is to be found in the statement of Lord Bramwell in *Leigh v Jack* ((1879) 5 Ex. D. 264):

> "Acts of user are not enough to take the soil out of the Plaintiff and, and vest it in the Defendant; in order to defeat a title by dispossessing and the former owner, acts must be done which are inconsistent with the [sic] his enjoyment of the soil, for the purposes for which he intended to use it."

In that case, land was acquired for the purpose of a future street. It was intended to lay idle in the meantime. The defendant used the land to store scrap metal. It was held that the plaintiff had not been dispossessed/had not discontinued possession. It was also held that there was no *animus possidendi* on the part of the defendant. He knew that the land was intended for future use, and his use was not inconsistent with that future use.

The rule in *Leigh v Jack* has now been rejected by the United Kingdom courts and was expressly disapproved by Barron J. in *Durack (Seamus) Manufacturing v Considine* ([1987] I.R. 677). In that case, the plaintiffs' predecessors in title had purchased two fields to build a factory. Only one of the fields housed the factory. The defendant began to graze cattle in the unoccupied field and fenced around it. It was argued that the defendant's possession was not adverse because it was not inconsistent with the purpose for which the owner intended to use the land. The judge held that this point only went to negative an *animus possidendi* when there was actual knowledge by the squatter of the owner's future intentions in relation to the land:

"Adverse possession depends on the existence of animus possidendi and it is the presence or absence of this state of mind which must be determined. Where no use is being made of the land and the claimant knows that the owner intends to use it for a specific purpose in the future, this is a factor to be taken into account. The principle has relevance only insofar as that when this factor is present it is easier to hold an absence of animus possidendi. An awareness of the landowner's intention was a factor which might make it reasonable to infer that there was no animus possidendi ... the intention of the landowner had no other relevance to the issue of whether there had been adverse possession".

However, despite the above dictum of Barron J., *Leigh v Jack* was subsequently applied by Egan J. in *Cork Corporation v Lynch* ([1995] 2 I.L.R.M. 598). A plot of land had been acquired by the plaintiffs with the intention that it should be used as part of a road development. The defendant owned a neighbouring garage and started to park cars on the plaintiff's land. He fenced around the plot and resurfaced it. There was held to be no adverse possession insofar as the defendant's occupation was not inconsistent with an intention of the local authority to use the land for road widening. In addition, Finnegan J., in *Feehan v Leamy*, endorsed Cockburn C.J.'s dicta in *Leigh v Jack* that the intention to possess was not met where there was simply a usage "until the time should come for carrying out the objective originally contemplated" by the owner.

The conflict between the Irish authorities was expressly considered by Clarke J. in *Dunne v Iarnród Éireann* ([2007] IEHC 314), in which he stated as follows:

"It has been suggested that there are two lines of authority in relation to adverse possession in this jurisdiction. One is said to derive from the judgment of Egan J. in Cork Corporation v. Lynch (Unreported, High Court, 26th July, 1985, Egan J.) in which the English case of Leigh v. Jack [1879] 5 Ex. D. 264 was followed. On that basis, the fact that a statutory body had a future intention to use lands which had been compulsorily acquired for the purposes of a public undertaking was held to defeat the possibility of adverse possession given that the statutory body concerned had no immediate use for the lands until such time as the statutory undertaking was to take place ... However, I prefer the reasoning of Barron J. in Durack Manufacturing in which he accepted that factors such as the future intended use of the property by the party with paper title might be a factor in determining whether the necessary intention was present in the party claiming adverse possession but was not otherwise a matter properly taken into account. As I understand the judgment of Barron J. it is to the effect that it might be inferred that a person, knowing that the paper title owner had no present use for the land but had a future use for it, might occupy it, not for the purposes of possessing it absolutely, but rather for the purposes of making temporary use of it until such time as the future purpose came on stream. In those circumstances the possessing party might not have a sufficient intention to dispossess the owner. In fairness, counsel for CIE agreed that, on the facts of this case, there was no evidence that CIE had, for much of the relevant period, an identified future purpose for the lands that could have allowed reliance on Cork Corporation v. Lynch in any event."

However, it appears that, given the conflicting High Court authorities, the matter will not be finally resolved until a Supreme Court judgment issues on this point.

II. DEFENCES TO CLAIMS OF ADVERSE POSSESSION

The 1957 Act provides for a number of defences to adverse possession claims. Time may stop running against the owner if there is a written and signed acknowledgment by the squatter of the owner's rights, or if there have been payments from the squatter to the owner. If the owner is under a disability such as infancy or insanity, time does not run against him during the period of disability. However, a squatter who has been in adverse possession for the requisite 12 years during the period of disability only has to show six subsequent years' adverse possession in order to extinguish the title. Finally, fraud and/or mistake may defeat a claim to have extinguished title by adverse possession.

i) ACKNOWLEDGMENT

Sections 51 and 58 of the 1957 Act state that where there has accrued to any person (other than a mortgagee) any right of action to recover land, and the person in possession of the land or his agent acknowledges the title of the person to whom the right of action has accrued, the right of action shall be deemed to have accrued on and not before the date of the acknowledgment. This has the effect that any adverse possession accruing prior to the acknowledgment (except adverse possession which has already succeeded in extinguishing title at the time of the acknowledgment) should be discounted.

An acknowledgment for this purpose must be in writing, signed by the person making the acknowledgment or his agent, and made to the person or the agent of the person whose title, right, equity of redemption or claim is being acknowledged. However, it should be noted that an oral acknowledgment may defeat *animus possidendi*.

In *Edginton v Clark* ([1964] 1 Q.B. 367) an offer by a squatter to buy the property on which they were squatting was held to be an acknowledgment on the basis that, "if a man makes an offer to purchase freehold property, even though it be subject to contract, he is quite clearly saying that as between himself and the person to whom he makes the offer, he realises that the offeree has a better title to the freehold land than himself, and that would seem to be the plainest possible form of acknowledgment." This mirrors the approach taken in the earlier case of *Johnston v Smith* ([1896] I.R. 83) in which a written proposal by an over holding tenant to purchase the property was held to constitute an acknowledgment of his landlord's title so as to stop time running against the landlord for the purpose of the 1957 Act.

However, not all offers to purchase the rightful owners' interest will necessarily constitute acknowledgments. In *Doe d Curzon v Edmonds* ((1840) 6 M. & W. 295) (approved in *Edginton*), a letter from a squatter stating that, although he was satisfied that he would establish a legal right to the premises, he was agreeable to pay a moderate rent on an agreement for 21 years, was held not to constitute an acknowledgment.

In *Ofulue v Bossert* ([2008] EWCA Civ 7) it was recently held that a written offer to buy disputed property, made on an expressly without prejudice basis for the purposes of resolving an ongoing dispute in relation to that property, did not constitute an acknowledgment. It appears that the rationale for this decision was the fact that the offer was made expressly without prejudice and in the context of existing or pending court proceedings, so that treating it as an acknowledgment would detrimentally affect the public interest in resolving disputes.

ii) Fraud

Section 71(1) of the 1957 Act provides that where, in the case of an action for which a period of limitation is fixed by the Act, either (a) the action is based on the fraud of the defendant or his agent or of any person through whom he claims or his agent, or (b) the right of action is concealed by the fraud of any such person, the period of limitation shall not begin to run until the plaintiff has discovered the fraud or could with reasonable diligence have discovered it.

However, this defence cannot be raised against a purchaser from the fraudulent squatter without notice of the fraud. Section 71(2) states that nothing in subs.(1) of this section shall enable an action to be brought to recover, or enforce any charge against, or set aside any transaction affecting, any property which has been purchased for valuable consideration by a person who was not a party to the fraud and did not at the time of the purchase know or have reason to believe that any fraud had been committed.

iii) Disability

Section 49(1)(a) of the 1957 Act provides that if, on the date of accrual of the relevant right of action, the person to whom it accrued was under a disability, the action may, subject to the subsequent provisions of this section, be brought at any time before the expiration of six years from the date when the person ceased to be under a disability or died, whichever event first occurred notwithstanding that the period of limitation has expired. There is a long stop provision of 30 years.

Persons under a disability are defined in s.48 as infants, persons of unsound mind or convicts subject to the operation of the Forfeiture Act 1870, in whose case no administrator or curator has been appointed under that Act. Section 48(2) states that a person shall be conclusively presumed to be of unsound mind while he is detained in pursuance of any enactment authorising the detention of persons of unsound mind or criminal lunatics.

In the case of such persons, their title is not extinguished on expiration of the normal 12-year period but continues until either six years from the date of cessation of the disability or death or 30 years, whichever is the earlier. Section 49 further provides that where a right of action which has accrued to a person under a disability accrues, on the death of that person while still under a disability, to another person under a disability, no further extension of time shall be allowed by reason of the disability of the second person.

III. Effect of Extinguishment of Title

If the requirements for adverse possession are satisfied throughout the requisite period, as appropriate, and none of the defences apply, the title of the dispossessed owner is extinguished.

However, there may be other persons entitled to ownership rights in the land, e.g. landlords/remaindermen, whose title has not been extinguished. The extent of any possessory title acquired by the squatter lasts, at most, for the duration of the title of the dispossessed owner. If the dispossessed owner is a leaseholder, at best (assuming that the landlord does not exercise his right of forfeiture as discussed below) the squatter has an entitlement to stay on for the duration of the lease. If the dispossessed owner is a life tenant, tenant in tail, or tenant *pur autre vie*, the squatter has an entitlement to stay on for the duration of the life estate, fee tail or estate *pur autre vie* only.

It is also important to note that, although the squatter's possessory title is limited by reference to the title of the dispossessed owner, he does not actually get a conveyance of the dispossessed owner's title either in law or in equity. All he gets is a possessory title limited to the period of the dispossessed owner's title.

In the last century, a different view was taken, and it was thought that adverse possession operated to convey of the title of the dispossessed owner to the squatter at the end of the relevant period. The Irish case of *Rankin v Mc Murtry* ((1889) 24 L.R.T. Ir. 290) supported the parliamentary conveyance theory but this was rejected in *Tichborne v Weir* ((1892) 67 L.T. 735) and *O'Connor v Foley* ([1906] 1 I.R. 20).

It was agreed by the Supreme Court in *Perry v Woodfarm Homes Ltd* ([1975] I.R. 104) that the parliamentary conveyance theory was no longer valid and that adverse possession only operated to extinguish the rights of the dispossessed owner and did not transfer any de jure rights to the squatter. However, by virtue of his possession, the squatter has a claim over the land superior to that of anyone who subsequently goes into possession, and which can only be challenged by someone with legal or equitable title.

This right stemming from possession is known as the *jus possidendi*. If the only person who can prove a legal or equitable title is the person whose rights have been extinguished, then there is no one who can oust the squatter. Even if he ceases possession of the land and another person (the second squatter) goes into occupation without his permission, the prior possession of the first squatter will prevail against this person. It would require 12 years' adverse possession by the second squatter before this possessory title would come to an end. A possessory title may be transferred inter vivos or pass under a will or intestacy and, as stated above, extinguished by the 1957 Act in the same way as a paper title.

The rejection of the parliamentary conveyance theory has had some important side effects for the doctrine of adverse possession in this jurisdiction. First, it is unclear whether or not the squatter gets the benefit of easements previously enjoyed by the dispossessed owner. It appears clear that, if the squatter obtains adverse possession to part of the land of the dispossessed owner only, he does not acquire any implied easements, even easements of necessity, and will have to rely on the doctrine of prescription in this regard.

However, the rejection of the parliamentary conveyance theory has had greatest significance in the context of adverse possession of leasehold land. It means that the squatter does not get the benefit of the tenant's entitlements under the lease. In particular, there is no obligation on the landlord to ensure that he has quiet enjoyment of the land, nor is there any obligation on the part of the landlord to accept rent from him. In addition, the squatter has no entitlement to see the lease and familiarise himself with the obligations of the tenant. The problems arising from same are discussed in Section V below.

Finally, it would appear that a squatter on land can improve his position in this regard by registering a possessory title to that land. The wording of the Registration of Title Act 1964 (the "1964 Act") indicates that registration with a possessory title has the effect of a parliamentary conveyance.

IV. Special Situations of Adverse Possession

i) Adverse possession and leasehold land

This issue, which has been touched upon at various points in the previous sections, encompasses four different situations: (a) adverse possession of the property the subject of the lease by a stranger against a tenant; (b) adverse possession of the said property by a stranger against a landlord; (c) adverse possession of the said property by a tenant against a landlord; and (d) adverse possession by a tenant of land adjoining the property the subject of the lease and owned by the same landlord, a different tenant of the same landlord or a stranger.

(a) Adverse possession by a stranger against a tenant

The rejection of the parliamentary conveyance theory creates particular difficulties for squatters on leasehold land. In particular, they are at risk of early determination of the lease, perhaps by the landlord in collusion with the dispossessed tenant. In *Fairweather v St. Marylebone Property Co. Ltd* ([1963] A.C. 510), the House of Lords held that the dispossessed tenant, although he no longer had a right to sue the squatter, had a right under the lease which he could use to terminate the lease by surrender or merger. The word "extinguished" in the statute should be read as "extinguished against the squatter" rather than against the landlord. This conclusion was reached on a very circuitous interpretation of the statutory provisions and was rejected by the Supreme Court in *Perry v Woodfarm Homes Ltd.*

However, the Supreme Court in *Perry* did recognise that although the squatter could not be removed by surrender or merger, he could be removed by a forfeiture effected by the landlord on the basis of non-payment of rent/breaches of covenant. Because of the rejction of the parliamentary conveyance theory, the landlord is not obliged to accept rent from the squatter nor is he obliged to make him aware of the covenants in the lease. As Lord Denning points out in *Fairweather*, it is as easy for a landlord to organise a forfeiture as it is to organise a surrender or a merger. He merely has to refuse to accept rent from the squatter. This makes matters very uncertain for a squatter on leasehold land, and the Law Reform Commission has recommended restoration of the parliamentary conveyance theory for this reason.

It would appear that a squatter on leasehold land can improve his position by having himself registered with a possessory leasehold title insofar as the wording of the 1964 Act indicates that registration with a possessory title has the effect of a parliamentary conveyance. Until recently, this facility was not available where the leasehold interest of the dispossessed owner was unregistered; the Land Registry would only permit registration of a possessory title to a leasehold interest where that leasehold interest was already registered or (in exceptional circumstances) in cases of adverse possession as between family members. However, the position has improved in this regard following the enactment of the Registration of Deeds and Title Act 2006, s.50(d) of which amends s.3 of the 1964 Act to provide for registration of first leasehold interests acquired by long possession.

(b) Adverse possession by a stranger against a landlord

As stated above, since time does not begin to run against a landlord until the lease comes to an end, adverse possession by a squatter on leasehold land does not extinguish the landlord's interest, nor does it extinguish the lease or tenancy, which continues to subsist. This interest can only be extinguished by the squatter continuing in adverse possession for 12 years following the determination of the lease or tenancy.

(c) Adverse possession by a tenant against a landlord (in respect of the property the subject of the lease or tenancy)

A tenant who continues in occupation of the property the subject of the lease for 12 years following the determination of his lease or tenancy will extinguish the landlord's interest by adverse possession. It should be noted that, under s.17(2) of the 1957 Act, non-payment of rent will extinguish an oral periodic tenancy, without the need for a notice to quit (although subsequent payment and acceptance of rent within the 12-year period will resurrect the tenancy). Non-payment of rent, however, will not determine a fixed-term lease or written periodic tenancy.

It should also be noted that, because of the provisions in s.17 of the 1957 Act, a tenant who stays on after the expiration of a fixed-term lease with oral permission and thereby becomes a tenancy at will subsequently becomes a squatter after one year unless the permission is renewed or rent is accepted.

(d) Adverse possession by a tenant against adjoining property owned by his landlord or by a third party

The presumption in this case, as set out in *King v Smith* ([1950] 1 All E.R. 553), is that the occupation of the adjoining land by the tenant is in his capacity as tenant of the leasehold land and (subject to the lease) for the benefit of his landlord. In other words, the tenant's possessory title to the adjoining land becomes subject to the covenants and conditions in the lease, including rent review provisions, and reverts to his landlord on termination of the lease. This principle, which is known as the doctrine of encroachment, applies whether the adjoining land belongs to the landlord, is occupied by another tenant of the same landlord or is owned by a third party. Roxburgh J. in *King* stated that this presumption could be rebutted by proving that the landlord and tenant so conducted themselves as to show that the landlord did not regard the encroachment as for his benefit.

ii) ADVERSE POSSESSION AND PROPERTY FORMING PART OF THE ESTATE OF A DECEASED PERSON

Again, three different situations arise here: (a) adverse possession by a third party; (b) adverse possession by a personal representative; (c) adverse possession by one or some of the persons entitled.

(a) Adverse possession of property forming part of a deceased's estate by a third party

The time limit for the personal representatives to bring actions on behalf of the estate against this third party is 12 years from the date the right of action first accrued by virtue of s.13(2)(a) of the 1957 Act. If the adverse possession commenced before the deceased's death, the personal representatives will have less than 12 years in which to bring a claim. If the adverse possession commenced 12 years or more before the deceased's death, it would appear that the deceased's title to the property was extinguished at the date of his death and, as such, it does not form part of his estate.

The continuing application of the 12-year period to personal representatives was cast into some doubt by s.126 of the 1965 Act, which provides that in the case of deaths occurring after the coming into effect of the 1965 Act, no action in respect of any claim to the estate of a deceased person or to any share or interest in such estate, whether under a will, on intestacy or under s.111 of the 1965 Act, shall be brought after the expiration of six years from the date when the right to receive the share or interest accrued.

However, it was held in *Drohan v Drohan* ([1984] I.L.R.M. 179), subsequently affirmed by the Supreme Court in *Gleeson v Feehan* ([1991] I.L.R.M.

783), that s.126 does not apply to claims by personal representatives to recover possession and that such claims are governed by the 12-year limitation period in s.13(2)(a).

(b) Adverse possession by a personal representative of property forming part of a deceased's estate

Originally, a personal representative was regarded as being in the position of express trustee and could not bar the title of the beneficiaries to the property of the deceased. However, in *Vaughan v Cottingham* ([1961] I.R. 184), the Supreme Court decided that a personal representative was not an express trustee for the beneficiaries in relation to registered land and consequently s/he could, as trustee, bar the beneficiaries by 20 years' adverse possession by virtue of s.13 of the Law of Property Amendment Act 1860. The Administration of Estates Act 1959 changed the law in this regard by providing that in respect of deaths after January 1, 1959 adverse possession by the personal representatives for a period of 12 years would operate to bar the claims of the beneficiaries.

Section 126 of the 1965 Act reduces this period to six years from the date on which the beneficiary's right to receive their share and interest accrues. Section 126 applies in respect of deaths after January 1, 1967.

It is possible that if the personal representative in adverse possession were replaced, the new personal representative could then bring a claim against them relying on the 12-year period discussed at (a) above. However, the capacity of the beneficiaries to have the personal representative replaced once their share has been extinguished under s.126 is unclear.

(c) Adverse possession of property forming part of a deceased's estate by one or some of the persons entitled

This often occurs on an intestacy, where some of the children remain on or return to the land and others vacate it. As stated above, 12 years' adverse possession is required in order to bar the entitlement of the personal representatives to recover possession.

One issue which arises where there are a number of beneficiaries/heirs on intestacy in possession is the nature of the possessory co-ownership acquired by them. Prior to the 1965 Act such persons held as tenants in common between themselves and after the limitation had elapsed acquired the interests of those who remained away as joint tenants (*Smith v Savage* ([1906] 1 I.R. 469)).

Section 125 of the 1965 Act provides that where each of two or more persons is entitled to any share in land comprised in the estate of a deceased person, whether such shares are equal or unequal, and any or all of them enter into possession of the land, then, notwithstanding any rule of law to the contrary, those who enter shall (as between themselves and as between themselves and those (if any) who do not enter) be deemed, for the purposes of the 1957 Act, to have entered and to have acquired title by possession as joint tenants (and not as tenants in common) as regards their own respective shares and also as regards the respective shares of those (if any) who do not enter. Subsection 2 of the same section provides that subs.(1) shall apply whether or not any such person entered into possession as personal representative of the deceased, or having entered, was subsequently granted representation to the estate of the deceased.

In *Gleeson v Purcell* ([1997] I.L.R.M. 522) it was held that the effect of this section as regards deaths following the coming into effect of the 1965 Act was to make those heirs who took possession hold as joint tenants and to enable them to acquire the interests of those who remain away as joint tenants.

12 Succession Law

Succession law deals with what happens to an individual's property when he or she dies. It regulates the transfer of a person's real and personal property on their death. To the extent that succession law deals with the transfer of personal property on death, it goes beyond the strict confines of a land law course, which would deal with the law of real property only. However, the rules for transfer of real and personal property on death are similar and are commonly taught together as part of a land law course. This is how they will be dealt with here.

There are two different sets of rules for distributing an individual's property on his or her death. Which set of rules is applied depends on whether the individual has made a will or not. A will is a document made by the deceased directing the distribution of his property in a particular way after his or her death. If an individual has made a valid will, he or she dies testate. His or her property is divided according to the terms of his will, with some potential statutory modifications.

For example, if an individual does not leave his property to his family in his will, leaving his wife destitute and his children poverty-stricken, this can be remedied by the wife and children invoking the rights conferred on them by Pt IX of the Succession Act 1965 (the "1965 Act"). To this extent, statutory provisions may override the terms of a will.

On an entirely different issue, if an individual dies without having made a valid will, he dies intestate. His property is divided according to the rules on intestate succession. These rules are laid down in the 1965 Act.

I. WILLS

A will is a disposition executed by an individual in which he outlines the way in which he would like his property to be distributed on his death. The person making the will is known as the testator (male) or the testatrix (female).

There is obviously a risk of forged wills, and so certain formal requirements have been introduced to prevent this. If a will does not satisfy these, it cannot be enforced and the result is that the deceased dies intestate (without a valid will) and the rules on intestacy have to be applied.

REQUIREMENTS FOR A VALID WILL

(a) Capacity

This means that the testator (the person making the will) must be of sound mind and of age (over the age of 18, or married).

In *Blackall v Blackall* (unreported, Supreme Court, April 1, 1998) and *O Donnell v O Donnell* (unreported, High Court, Kelly J., March 24, 1999) both challenges were rejected. Kelly J. in the latter case quoted from the High Court judgment of McCracken J. in *Blackall* (unreported, High Court, McCracken J., June 28, 1996) which had been affirmed by the Supreme Court.

McCracken J. stated as follows:

> "The onus of proving the formal validity of a will is undoubtedly on the person who propounds the will, but where there is a challenge to a will based on the state of knowledge or state of health of the testator, the onus is on the person who challenges the will."

The testator in *O Donnell* had been a paranoid schizophrenic for many years. However, Kelly J. accepted medical evidence to the effect that his condition was both controllable and controlled by medication. The fact that the deceased was eccentric in some respects did not mean that he was incapable of making a will. Remarks that the deceased made to his solicitor at the time of signing the will displayed considerable insight and were absolutely accurate. The will itself was rational, clear, insightful and sensible. The presumption of sound disposing mind had not been rebutted.

(b) Formal requirements

1. Writing

The 1965 Act mirrors previous legislation by requiring that a will be in writing, signed at the bottom by the testator, and that his signature be made or acknowlegded in the presence of two witnesses both present at the same time, who sign to verify this.

N.B. A will made by tape recorder, or video tape, is not valid because it is not in writing, even though it is recorded on a permanent record.

2. The will must be signed by the testator, or by someone directed by him

Placing of the signature: The signature must be at the foot of the will. Any substantive provisions which follow the signature will make it invalid. However, the 1965 Act provides that a space may intervene between the foot of the will or the signature, and that the signature may be on a separate page at the end of the will.

The signature itself:

- The signature does not have to be legible. This was established by *In b. Kieran* ([1933] I.R. 22).

- Any mark made by the testator intended by him as his signature can qualify as his signature. This is important for illiterate testators. In the case of *Re Glynn* ([1990] 2 I.R. 326) an "X" was held sufficient.

- Sometimes the testator may not sign his real name but may use a nickname or family name by which he is generally known, e.g. "Your Loving Mother", as occurred in *In b. Cook* ([1960] 1 W.L.R. 353). This too is permissible.

- The 1965 Act provides that the testator may direct someone else to sign the will on his behalf, e.g. if he is too weak to sign. It has been stated in *In b. McLoughlin* ([1936] I.R. 223) that it is acceptable for the person so directed to sign not in the testator's name but in his own name. If the person directed signs the testator's name, it is uncertain whether the will is invalid or not. The direction to the signing person by the testator must be made in the presence of witnesses.

- Sometimes the testator has to be aided to write his signature by someone else, e.g. a nurse's help is needed to aid him in moving the pen. In *Fulton v Kee* ([1961] N.I. 1) it was held that the assisted mark counts as the signature of the testator provided that he made an independent physical contribution to the making of the mark. Even if he did not make an independent physical contribution, it is arguable that the signature was valid on the grounds that he impliedly directed the nurse to sign for him in the event that he was unable to do so.

The judicial interpretation of the signature requirement has been quite flexible. The reason for this is that a further rule exists to safeguard the testator. The witnessing requirements require that the testator either make or acknowledge the signature as his in the presence of two witnesses. Thus, an illegible mark may constitute a signature, but it will not ground a valid will unless made in front of witnesses.

3. The will must be witnessed

- There must be two or more witnesses. The signature must be either made or acknowledged in the presence of both witnesses who must then sign the will to say that they have witnessed this. Again, initials or a mark will suffice as the witness's signature.

- The witnesses do not have to, and usually do not, see the contents of the will. What often happens is that the substantive part of the will is covered over with a page, with only the signature at the bottom showing. The testator either makes this signature in the presence of the witnesses, or acknowledges it as his own in their presence. Then they sign to say that they have witnessed the signature. The witness's signature does not have to be under the testator's signature and can be on any part of the will.

- The witness must actually see the signing or acknowledgment of the signature. A blind person cannot be a valid witness. Similarly, a witness whose path of vision is obscured at the crucial moment of signature or acknowledgment cannot be a valid witness.

- The witness requirements are a crucial part of the formality requirements, particularly given the fact that the signature requirements are so flexible. For this reason it is important that a witness's signature be genuine and not be influenced by any considerations of personal gain. Therefore, a witness cannot receive any gift under a will they have witnessed. Any gifts to witnesses or to the spouses of witnesses are void. It is important to note that the chosen solution in this case is not to make the will invalid, but to render the gifts to the witnesses void. This rule is illustrated by the case of *Re Bravda* ([1968] 1 W.L.R. 479). A father executed a will leaving his property between his two daughters. There were four witnesses to the will, two of whom unfortunately were the daughters. For this reason the gifts to the daughters were invalid. It did not matter that they were superfluous witnesses.

- However, if the gift to the witness is a gift to the witness as trustee, or if the gift is on its face to someone else but the witness takes as beneficiary under a secret trust (a trust *dehors* the will), the gift is valid.

ADDITIONS AND CHANGES TO A WILL

It is a core principle of the 1965 Act that anything which comes after the signature is void. This includes provisions which come after the signature in time, as well as those provisions which come after it in the document itself. Therefore, any crossings out on the will which take place subject to the testator's signature are void. There is a presumption that any alterations to the body of the will have taken place after signature and therefore are invalid. This presumption may be rebutted.

If a testator wishes to make alterations to his will he may do this in one of three ways:

1. He may revoke the original will and execute an entirely new one.
2. He may execute a codicil or supplementary provision to the will containing the alterations. To be valid, this codicil must be signed and witnessed although the witnesses do not have to be the same as the witnesses to the original will.
3. He may write the alterations in on the original will. However, each individual alteration must be signed and witnessed.

REVOKING A WILL

Express revocation may be achieved either by executing a formal document which states that it is revoking the will, or by some act of revocation, e.g. destruction of the will with the intention to revoke. N.B. Mere destruction of the will per se will not constitute a revocation unless such destruction is coupled with an intention on the part of the testator to revoke.

A will is automatically revoked on marriage or registration of civil partnership and may be revoked if a completely new will is made, the terms of which are inconsistent with that of the previous will.

Once a will is revoked, it can never be revived. The only way around this is to execute a new will.

ADMINISTRATION OF A WILL

Assume the existence of a valid will, which has not been revoked at any time before the testator's death. We now have to consider how the estate of someone who dies testate is administered on their death.

On the death of a testator, his property automatically vests in the persons named as executors in the will, to be distributed by them to the beneficiaries named in the will. The executors have to apply for a grant of representation before they can administer the property. This process of applying for a grant of representation is also known as proving the will, admitting the will to probate, or getting a grant of probate.

If a will has been lost, its contents may be reconstructed by the court, provided that it has not been revoked by destruction.

Representation will only be granted by the court/probate office if they are satisfied that there is a valid will.

If there is nobody named as executor under the will, or the person named as executor declines his duties, or the deceased dies intestate, then the property of the deceased vests in the Master of the High Court until such time as administrators are appointed. The beneficiaries under the will or on intestacy should apply to the court for a grant of representation to ask the court to appoint administrators. This is known as applying for letters of administration. Once letters of administration have been granted, the newly appointed administrators have the same rights and duties as executors who have been given a grant of representation. Both executors and administrators may be described as the deceased's personal representatives and they shall be referred to together under this title hereafter.

Once a grant of representation/letters of administration have been made, the deceased's property devolves to the personal representatives and the process of dealing with his estate begins. Personal representatives will get custody of all the documents of title and will pay off all debts. The 1965 Act lays down the order in which certain debts or liabilities should be paid off.

After paying off the debts of the deceased, the question of distributing his property to the beneficiaries under his will or on intestacy arises. The personal representative has a general obligation to distribute the estate as soon as possible after the deceased's death. As stated already, the property of a deceased person vests on the personal representatives on death, or when letters of administration are granted, and they are stated to hold the estate as trustees for the persons who are entitled to it. This does not mean that the beneficiaries under the will or intestacy have a beneficial interest in the property while it is in the hands of the personal representatives. The personal representatives own the property absolutely, and are merely subject to a fiduciary obligation in respect thereof.

Personal representatives are entitled to sell any assets of the estate for the purposes of paying debts or distributing the estate among persons who are entitled to it. But if someone is specifically entitled to the asset under the will, the personal representatives must, so far as practicable, give effect to such an individual's wishes. They also have a right of appropriation. Under s.55 they may apply a specific item of property in its existing form towards the satisfaction of a person's share in the estate. However, an appropriation of this nature cannot affect any specific devise or bequest. The court may, at its discretion, prohibit the appropriation on the application of any one of the persons entitled under the will.

Often the personal representatives will have difficulty ascertaining from the terms of a will which individuals are meant to benefit. The following principles are helpful.

INTERPRETATION OF WILLS

A will speaks from death

When interpreting a will, one does not look at the situation at the time the will was made, but rather the situation at the time the testator died. Therefore, property which was acquired by the testator after he made the will may still be distributed under the will. In addition, gifts to people who predeceased the testator are invalid and fall into the residue if there is a residue clause, or otherwise fall to be distributed on intestacy (a partial intestacy). This is known as the doctrine of lapse.

There is one exception to the doctrine of lapse: if a parent makes a gift to their child, who dies before them, and that child has issue living at the time of the grandparent's death, the gift does not lapse (s.98 of the 1965 Act). This principle was applied in *Moorehead v Tiilikainen* ([1999] 2 I.L.R.M. 471) where a daughter predeceased her mother. However, the result in this case probably conflicted with the policy of s.98 to some extent. The daughter died intestate and her husband received two-thirds of the gift made to her by her mother. The three grandchildren merely received one-ninth of the gift each.

The "armchair principle"

When the court is interpreting a will it must put itself in the same position as the testator, see the world through his eyes, and be aware of the phrases he used in his lifetime to describe things. This is known as the "armchair principle": the judge must sit in the testator's chair, and get within his mindset.

An example of the application of the armchair principle can be found in *Thorn v Dickens* ([1906] W.N. 54). Here a testator left all his property to "mother". Evidence was admitted that he had been in the habit of using the term "mother" to refer to his wife.

The armchair principle primarily relates to the testator's use of language. If there is evidence that the testator was in the habit of using a particular word to refer to a particular person or thing during his lifetime, and he has used this word in his will, evidence can be admitted that he used this word to refer to a particular person or thing. So the scope for admission of evidence under the armchair principle is quite limited. The limits of the armchair principle were shown in *Re Julian* ([1950] I.R. 57).

Re Julian involved an interpretation of the will of an old lady who had left her money to the Seamen's Institute, Sir John Rogerson's Quay, Dublin. The testatrix was a Protestant and the only Seamen's Institute at Sir John Rogerson's Quay was the Catholic Seamen's Institute. There was a Protestant Seamen's Institute located on Eden Quay. Evidence was sought to be admitted that when the old lady was drawing up her will she asked her lawyer for the address of the Protestant Seamen's Institute. He looked up the directory, and saw only one institute listed, the Seamen's Institute, Sir John Rogerson's Quay. So he put this title and address down.

However, it was held that evidence of the circumstances surrounding the making of the will was not admissible. First of all, the armchair principle was ineffective in the circumstances of the case.

There was an alternative, broader principle in the law suggesting that extrinsic evidence of circumstances surrounding the making of the will generally could be admitted in cases of ambiguity. The trial judge in *Re Julian* (and this is a much argued point) appeared to say that there was an ambiguity on the facts, but that the common law principle only allowed extrinsic evidence in respect of a particular type of ambiguity, and that the ambiguity in *Re Julian* was not of this type. It was not a description which applied equally to two things, but one which applied partly to one thing and partly to another, but wholly accurately to neither. Extrinsic evidence was not admissible to resolve the latter kind of ambiguity.

Extrinsic evidence and s.90 of the Succession Act 1965

Subsequent to *Re Julian* the 1965 Act was enacted and s.90 provided as follows:

> Extrinsic evidence shall be admissible to show the intention of the testator and to assist in the construction of, or to explain any contradiction in, a will.

Did this provision change the law in *Re Julian*? The issue has been discussed by Irish courts in a number of post-1965 cases.

First, in *Rowe v Law* ([1978] I.R. 55), the Supreme Court was called upon to decide whether extrinsic evidence could be admitted to change the contents of a will even where there was no ambiguity on the face of the will. The answer of the majority of the Supreme Court was in the negative. O'Higgins C.J. delivered a strong dissent.

The three arguments voiced by the majority in support of their conclusion were as follows:

(i) An interpretation of the wording of s.90 indicated that extrinsic evidence was only admissible in cases of ambiguity. With respect, this argument was incorrect.

(ii) Section 90 should be interpreted in the context of the 1965 Act as a whole.

(iii) Policy considerations.

Arguments (ii) and (iii) were the more compelling. Henchy J. feared that allowing widespread extrinsic evidence of intention would be a sweeping and disruptive change, fraught with possibilities for mistake and uncertainty. Griffin J. pointed out further dangers. Section 90 provided no controls on the admission of extrinsic evidence. Its terms did not restrict the admission of extrinsic evidence to documents made around the time of the making of the will. On the terms of s.90, evidence from years before or years after could be admitted. Section 90 should be controlled as much as possible.

In his dissent, O Higgins C.J. said that s.90 was clearly intended to enact a change in the law, and must be interpreted in this way. He felt that *Re Julian* would be decided the same way under the majority's interpretation of s.90; this destroyed any justification for enacting this section. He also based his conclusion on the wording of s.90.

Subsequent cases were *Lindsay v Tomlinson* (unreported, High Court, Carroll J., February 13, 1996) where there was a bequest to the National Society for the Prevention of Cruelty to Animals (Dogs and Cats Home), 1 Grand Canal Quay. This description did not fully apply to any existing body. There were two bodies to whom it partially applied: the Dublin Society for the Prevention of Cruelty to Animals and the Irish Society for the Prevention of Cruelty to Animals. It was held that there was an ambiguity and evidence could be given of the testator's relationship with the first institution throughout the last few years of her life in order to show that she intended to leave it to them.

However, in *Re Julian*, which was a very similar case, extrinsic evidence was not admissible. The judge in the case specifically said that the extrinsic evidence was being excluded, not because there was no ambiguity but because the ambiguity was not of the right type. To this extent, *Re Julian* could be decided otherwise today and s.90 did change it.

This was recognised by Keane J. in his very clear judgment in *Re Collins: O Connell v Bank of Ireland* ([1998] 2 I.R. 596). Here an attempt was made to get the Supreme Court to overrule *Rowe v Law*, relying on O Higgins C.J.'s minority reasoning in this case. However, as Keane J. pointed out, some of this reasoning was flawed. Section 90 was intended to effect, and did effect, a change in the law. In particular, he rejected O Higgins C.J.'s view that s.90 would have made no difference to the result in *Re Julian*. *Rowe v Law* was unequivocally affirmed, and the Supreme Court decision in *Re Curtin Deceased* ([1991] 2 I.R. 562), which some commentators had thought marked a departure from *Rowe*, was distinguished as an example of the application of the principle that a will should be construed in order to prevent an intestacy.

The position now is that extrinsic evidence may only be admitted if there is an ambiguity on the face of the will, for the purpose of resolving that ambiguity. In *Lynch v Burke* (unreported, High Court, McCracken J., July 30, 1999) the will was open to two different constructions. Extrinsic evidence was therefore admitted under s.90. However, on examination of the extrinsic evidence the judge found himself unable to take it into account in interpreting the will. The particular extrinsic evidence in hand did not support either of the alternative constructions. The language of the will would have to be severely stretched to give effect to the intention evidenced in the extrinsic evidence. It was felt that extrinsic evidence should only be used in interpreting a will if to do so would resolve an ambiguity. Here the extrinsic evidence did not resolve anything; it merely raised more problems and therefore it should be discounted.

Lynch v Burke illustrates the point that even if extrinsic evidence is admitted under s.90, and clearly shows the intention of the testator, it may on some occasions be impossible to interpret the will so as to give effect to that intention. Even when extrinsic evidence is admitted, it cannot be used so as to do violence to the language of the will.

II. Statutory Rights of Spouses/Civil Partners and Children under the Succession Act 1965

For centuries the principle of freedom of testation was inherent in the law. Then the 1965 Act introduced certain provisions to protect the family of a deceased. It gave both a spouse and a child of the deceased the right to override the terms of his will and to claim a share in the deceased's property to which they were not entitled under the will. This has recently been extended by the Civil Partnership and Certain Rights and Obligations of Cohabitants Act 2010 (the "2010 Act") to include civil partners, and even cohabitants.

In addition, the 1965 Act provided that a testator could not circumvent the terms of the 1965 Act by disposing of his property to others prior to his death. Section 121 applies to gifts of the testator's estate within the three years preceding his death. If the court finds that the disposition was made for the purpose of defeating or substantially diminishing the share of a person statutorily entitled, the court may order that the disposition may be deemed to be a bequest by will which forms part of the deceased's estate.

Spousal/civil partners' rights under section 111

(a) The spouse/civil partner of a deceased has a right to one-half of the deceased's estate if there are no children and one-third if there are children

Originally this applied to spouses only but has been extended by the 2010 Act to include parties in same-sex relationships who have registered as civil partners. Section 81 of the 2010 Act amends s.111 of the 1965 Act to provide that a surviving civil partner is, like a surviving spouse, entitled to a legal right share: one-third of the estate if there are children of the deceased or one-half if there are no children.

If the spouse/civil partner has been left nothing under the will, the spouse/civil partner automatically gets his or her legal right share.

If the spouse/civil partner has been left a gift under the will, they can choose either the gift or their legal right share. Usually the spouse/civil partner will choose whichever is larger in value. If the gift left to them under the will is lesser in value but has sentimental associations, they can take it in part-satisfaction of their legal right share. The 1965 Act states that a spouse/civil partner may elect to take any bequest given to them under the will in part-satisfaction of their legal right share.

However, when there is a gift under the will it is necessary for the spouse/civil partner to inform the personal representatives that they wish to take the legal right share instead of the gift under the will. They must positively elect in favour of the legal right share. If they fail to so inform them, they will only get the gift under the will. For this reason it is very important that the personal representatives notify the spouse/civil partner in writing of their right to elect for the legal right share.

This duty of positive election only arises where there is a gift to the spouse/civil partner under the will. If the spouse/civil partner gets nothing under the will, the legal right share vests automatically. There is no need for an election. This point was demonstrated by *O Dwyer v Keegan* ([1997] 2 I.L.R.M. 401). In this case a testator died 12 hours before his wife, to whom he had left nothing in his will. The question was whether the wife's heirs could claim her legal right share. The issue was whether the legal right share passed to her automatically on her husband's death, despite the fact that she was comatose at the time. The Supreme Court upheld the claim of the wife's heirs. She had obtained the legal right share automatically on her husband's death. The position would have been different had the husband left the wife a gift under the will.

It must also be noted that if a gift under a will is specifically expressed to be in addition to the legal right share, the spouse/civil partner will get both the gift under the will and the legal right share.

The legal right share is subject to one qualification in the case of civil partners: s.86 of the 2010 Act provides that, when deciding on a section 117 application by a child of the deceased civil partner, the court can reduce the legal right share of the surviving civil partner where necessary to correct a failure of moral duty on the part of the deceased. In deciding whether or not to exercise this power, the court shall consider all the circumstances, including the testator's financial circumstances and his or her obligations to the surviving civil partner, and shall only make an order reducing the share if it is of the opinion that it would be unjust not to make it. This contrasts with the position in relation to spouses, where a court has no jurisdiction, when dealing with a section 117 application by a child of a deceased, to reduce the legal right share of the spouse of the deceased.

(b) The right to compel the personal representatives to appropriate the dwelling-house

As well as his or her right to the legal right share, the surviving spouse/civil partner also has a right under s.56 of the 1965 Act and s.70 of the 2010 Act to compel the personal representatives to appropriate the dwelling-house in which they were living at the time of the deceased's death, and its contents, in satisfaction of their legal right share and/or the share of a dependant child under the will or s.117. Once again, the personal representatives have a duty to inform them of this right.

CHILDREN'S RIGHTS UNDER S.117

Unlike the legal right share, this right is not automatic, but depends on the discretion of the court. The provision itself is vague, and its operation has to be demonstrated by reference to case law.

Section 117 of the 1965 Act provides that where the court is of the opinion that the testator has failed in his moral duty to make proper provision for the child in accordance with his means, the court may order that just provision be made for the child out of the estate.

Child includes adopted and illegitimate children, and also children who are of age. The obligation under s.117 is not confined to minors nor to children of the deceased who were financially dependent on him.

An application under s.117 must be made within six months from the first taking out of representation of the deceased's estate. It cannot operate to reduce a gift made under the will to the testator's spouse, where that spouse is also the parent of the applicant. Where the spouse is a step-parent only, the section 117 application cannot reduce any gift made in the will to that step-parent below the level of the legal right share to which they would have been entitled under s.117.

Where a deceased dies leaving a civil partner rather than a spouse, the court has greater powers to give effect to rights under s.117. When deciding on a section 117 application by a child of the deceased civil partner, s.86 of the 2010 Act provides that the court can reduce the legal right share of the surviving civil partner where necessary to correct a failure of moral duty on the part of the deceased. In deciding whether or not to exercise this power, the court shall consider all the circumstances, including the testator's financial circumstances and his or her obligations to the surviving civil partner, and shall only make an order reducing the share if it is of the opinion that it would be unjust not to make it.

Whether a section 117 order will be granted depends on the following considerations laid down by Kenny J. in *Re G.M.* ((1972) 106 I.L.T.R. 82).

These guidelines were approved by the Supreme Court in *C.C. v W.C.* ([1990] 2 I.R. 143). The courts had to pay particular attention to the following factors:

- The number of the testator's children, their ages and positions in life.
- The means of the testator.
- The age of the applicant child.
- The children's financial position and prospects in life.
- Whether the testator had made financial provision for the applicant child during his life.

Taking into account the above factors, the testator must ask what a prudent and just parent would have done in this position. The standard is not that of the average parent, but of the prudent and just parent.

In *Re L.B.; E.B. v S.S.* ([1998] 2 I.L.R.M. 141) the plaintiff, aged 40, instituted proceedings under s.117, claiming that his mother had failed in her moral duty to provide for him. His mother who had died possessed a considerable estate and had left most of her estate to charity. The plaintiff had had problems with drugs in the past, was separated from his wife, was unemployed, and an alcoholic at the time of his mother's death. It was held that there had been no failure of moral duty on the part of the mother. The plaintiff's father, from whom the mother had inherited her property, had paid for him to go back to university when the plaintiff was in his late twenties. In addition, the plaintiff's father had provided him with a house in which he had lived with his family.

Keane J. stated that, in deciding the extent of the mother's moral duty, the circumstances at the time of her death were to be looked at. It was irrelevant that the plaintiff had subsequently beaten his addictions. In this case there was no failure of duty. The testatrix may have thought that the provision of money to her son in the past had had bad results. It was also stated that failure to provide for grandchildren can never be in breach of s.117 which only refers to a moral duty to children.

In *McDonald v Norris* ([2000] 1 I.L.R.M. 382) the section 117 applicant had had an acrimonious relationship with his father. He had been taken out of school aged 14 to work on the family farm when his father had been injured in an accident. He did all the work on the farm, his father receiving the profits except for the earnings from some acres of tillage and a quarry. The son received no wages. The father went to live with his sister-in-law's family and grew distant from the son after the son's marriage. He then tried to throw the son off the farm. The son refused to obey a court order to leave the farm and spent 12 months in prison for contempt. While he was in prison, the father gave some of the farm to his other son and sold yet another part. There was bad feeling against the father in the neighbourhood for his behaviour and the son did nothing to stop it. The father left all his property to his sister-in-law's child.

It was held that the son was entitled to what was left of the farm. The father had deprived his son of an education and a chance of an independent career. He had received the son's unpaid labour on the farm for many years. It was accepted that the son had to some extent failed in his moral duty towards his parent, and that his share under s.117 would reduce accordingly but the father's failure had been much greater. He had already financially provided for his in-laws during his life, so he could not be said to have been under a moral obligation to them at the time of his death. It was recognised that moral duties to third parties might be taken into account in reducing a child's share, although this had not been specifically stated in the section.

Barron J.'s Supreme Court judgment contrasts sharply with the High Court judgment of McCracken J. in the same case (reported at [1999] 1 I.L.R.M. 270). The two judges had differing views on who was most to blame for the unfortunate incidents which had occurred. They also had different opinions on whether the benefits which the son had received from the farm should be taken into account in assessing his share. It was stated by the Supreme Court that the kind of benefits, receipt of which would justify reducing a child's share under s.117, should relate to the funding of education, the provision of money or the transfer of property. The benefits received by the son were not of this nature.

There have been a number of subsequent decisions on s.117. In *DS v KM* (unreported, High Court, Carroll J., December 19, 2003), a testator died leaving two children, a son and a daughter. In his will he left his 40-acre farm and house to his son absolutely. He also left his son a further acre of land at M., subject to the proviso that his daughter could take a site from this portion of land for the purpose of building a house on it. Apart from this, the testator made no other gift to the daughter. The daughter brought a section 117 application claiming that the testator had failed in his moral duty to make proper provision for her in his will.

The testator's daughter, who suffered from diabetes, had always supported herself, but not in any lucrative employment. Her father had given her half the purchase price of her house and paid for her wedding. Apart from this he had made no other gifts to her. However, on the other hand, the testator's son suffered from a schizo-affective mental disorder and was receiving disability allowance. He had been admitted to mental hospital on four occasions and spent time in a local mental health hostel. A psychiatrist who gave evidence diagnosed him as requiring long-term treatment and support.

Carroll J. found that in the circumstances the gift of the property at M. to the son, subject to the daughter's right to build a house on it, was meaningless. The size of the site to be taken by the daughter was not defined. She noted that the entire acre of property was subject to a covenant, which precluded the property from being used for any purpose other than a single private dwelling house. This meant that if the daughter took any part of the property for the purposes of erecting a dwelling house, the son would be precluded from using the rest of the property for any purpose.

Given the special needs of the son, Carroll J. did not regard the bequest of the farm to the son as being in breach of the testator's moral duty. However, the bequest of the property at M. to the son was a different matter. The testator had failed in his moral duty by failing to leave the bequest of a viable site for his daughter. In the circumstances, it was the duty of the court under s.117 to achieve a distribution of the property between the children, which was in accordance with that moral duty:

> "The failure of the testator can be remedied by leaving the entire building site compromising approximately one acre of the lands at M — to DS. It then becomes an asset which she can sell if she wants. While it is only a small alteration to the will I consider that it achieves what the testator had in mind in making provision for his daughter. I do not believe that D's ability to continue his sheep farming will be affected in any way by this provision."

The testatrix in *K.C. v C.F.; M.C.* (unreported, High Court, Carroll J., December 16, 2003) died in 1999 leaving 11 surviving children. In her will she left the property to two of her sons, one of whom predeceased her. Two of the testatrix's daughters claimed that she had failed in her moral duty to make proper provision for them. One of these daughters, KC, had cared for the testatrix until her death and nursed her in her last illness. She had left school at 12 and never been in employment. Following her mother's death she had left the house and was currently living in a halting site. She had previously received £10,000 from her mother following the death of her father intestate. The other daughter, B.F.C., had left school at 15 and had been unemployed. She lived with her husband in local authority accommodation. She had never received any gift from her mother in her lifetime. Unlike her other siblings, she had not received any money from her mother following the death of her father intestate. The testatrix had paid for the weddings of her four married sons and gave each of them a van and caravan on their wedding.

Carroll J. held that there had been a failure of moral duty on the part of the mother in respect of the two daughters. As regards K.C., the £10,000 paid to her by the testatrix after the death of her father did not absolve the testatrix from her moral duty to make proper provision for her. B.F.C. had received no gifts from the testatrix during her lifetime. Carroll J. held that in deciding whether the moral duty to make proper provision had been fulfilled, the court should also take into account the position of "other children" of the testatrix, stating that:

> "[T]here are special circumstances which must be taken into account in this case. I do not think I can ignore those other children completely. M.C. has sworn an affidavit that he holds the money residue on a solemn trust for his brothers and sisters each to get 1/11th. Therefore, if he does follow through on this solemn trust which he has imposed upon himself (omitting K.C. and B.C.F.), the other brothers and sisters, while not beneficiaries under the will, will be affected by the exercise of the Court's powers … These are circumstances which I believe I must take into account and I cannot deal with the matter as if there were only K.C., B.C.F. and M.C. to consider. Neither can I deal with it on the basis that an eleventh share in the money residue is proper provision for either K.C. or B.C.F. This is not a case where an equal division of the residue would be fair … I am of opinion that K.C. is entitled to 200,000 and that B.F.C. is entitled to 100,000 out of the estate."

The most important recent judicial decision on s.117 is *In the Estate of ABC Deceased: XC, YC and ZC v RT, KU and JL* (unreported, High Court, Kearns J., April 2, 2003). The testator in this case had established a discretionary trust for the benefit of his children. Some of the children objected to same on the grounds that it did not discharge his moral duty under s.117 of the 1965 Act. Kearns J. rejected their claim and held that there was no failure of moral duty, listing the following legal principles which had been agreed by counsel *sub silentio* as applicable to s.117:

"(a) The social policy underlying Section 117 is primarily directed to protecting those children who are still of an age and situation in life where they might reasonably expect support from their parents against the failure of parents, who are unmindful of their duties in that area.

(b) What has to determined is whether the testator, at the time of his death, owes any moral obligation to the applicants and if so, whether he has failed in that obligation.

(c) There is a high onus of proof placed on an applicant for relief under Section 117 which requires the establishment of a positive failure in moral duty.

(d) Before a court can interfere there must be clear circumstances and a positive failure in moral duty must be established.

(e) The duty created by Section 117 is not absolute.

(f) The relationship of parent and child does not itself and without regard to other circumstances create a moral duty to leave anything by will to the child.

(g) Section 117 does not create an obligation to leave something to each child.

(h) The provision of an expensive education for a child may discharge the moral duty as may other gifts or settlements made during the lifetime of the testator.

(i) Financing a good education so as to give a child the best start in life possible, and providing money, which if properly managed, should afford a degree of financial security for the rest of one's life does amount to making proper provision.

(j) The duty under Section 117 is not to make adequate provision but to provide proper provision in accordance with the testator's means.

(k) A just parent must take into account not just his moral obligations to his children and to his wife, but all his moral obligations e.g. to aged and infirm parents.

(l) In dealing with a Section 117 application, the position of an applicant child is not to be taken in isolation. The court's duty is to consider the entirety of the testator's affairs and to decide upon the application in the overall context. In other words, while the moral claim of a child may require a testator to make a particular provision for him, the moral claims of others may require such provision to be reduced or omitted altogether.

(m) Special circumstances giving rise to a moral duty may arise if a child is induced to believe that by, for example, working on a farm he will ultimately become the owner of it thereby causing him to shape his upbringing, training and life accordingly.

(n) Another example of special circumstances might be a child who had a long illness or an exceptional talent which it would be morally wrong not to foster.

(o) Special needs would also include physical or mental disability.

(p) Although the court has very wide powers both as to when to make provisions for an applicant child and as to the nature of such provision such powers must not be construed as giving the court a power to make a new will for the testator.

(q) The test to be applied is not which of the alternative courses open to the testator the court itself would have adopted if confronted with the same situation but rather, whether the decision of the testator to opt for the course he did, of itself and without more, constituted a breach of moral duty to the plaintiff.

(r)   The court must not disregard the fact that parents must be presumed to know their children better than anyone else."

Applying these principles, he held that the testator had not failed in his duty to make proper provision for his children. He accepted that the deceased had been:

"[M]eticulous and exacting about accounting for expenditure, be it advances to the children for educational or house buying purposes, or to his two daughters and notably his older daughter, in connection with their wedding expenses. Both daughters feel, particularly Y, that the deceased some what spoiled these occasions by (in Y's case at least) requiring her to account for every single item of expenditure and refusing to underwrite the cost of champagne at the reception. However, when seen against the wider backdrop of the provision made for each of the girls, and bearing in mind the altered circumstances in which the deceased found himself, these complaints fall well short of amounting to any failure of moral duty to make proper provision. At the date of death of the deceased, his daughters were well established, had married and had their own homes. There were struggles along the way, both then and since, but both daughters have succeeded in life to a significant degree. Both are comfortably well off with considerable asset backing. Y has a career of her own and Z is married to a successful stockbroker in a leading Dublin firm."

As regards the testator's moral duty to his daughters:

"The court must consider moral duty as of the date of death of the testator. It is not in dispute that the testator had a moral duty to make adequate provision for the first named defendant [his second wife and the children's stepmother] and indeed his mother also who was in a nursing home. These moral duties must also be taken into account when assessing the moral duty owed by the testator to his children ... When one takes into account the various provisions made for both [his daughters] by the deceased during his lifetime and having regard to both his and their circumstances at the time of the testator's death, I am satisfied that he did, both by those provisions and by the further provisions in his will, discharge his moral duty in full towards his daughters."

In relation to the testator's son, X, the situation was more problematic.

"X has fallen on hard times and it would impossible not to feel a considerable measure of sympathy for his predicament. While he has a string of business failures, and has at times acted intemperately, notably with regard to his stepmother, he presented nonetheless as a decent person who grew up in the shadow of his father and who experienced great difficulty in trying to emulate his success. For reasons, therefore, which perhaps in no way reflect badly on him, he never became the kind of successful business man he undoubtedly aspired to be. It seems unlikely that any such ambitions, if he still harbours them, will ever now be realised."

Kearns J. concluded that a moral duty did exist in the case of X, but found that the testator had fulfilled this moral duty by establishing the discretionary trust, stating that:

"The deceased had little in the way of available cash and any direction to sell the residential properties in the immediate event of his death would have been folly. As the inflation in property values, including the unprecedented upsurge in the last few years, has demonstrated, the decision to place those assets under a trust arrangement, was a wise one, at least from the point of view of maximising the value of the assets … It must have been apparent to the testator, given the astute business-man that he was, that X was a person who would probably require a level of support at times in the future because of his inability to manage his affairs or to cope adequately in life … The duty to X was … in my view also discharged by the creation of a discretionary trust by the deceased's will, not least because it set in place, coincidentally or otherwise, the very apparatus and structure which was appropriate to meet the special needs which the deceased was clearly aware X had. Perhaps he could or should have selected different trustees. Perhaps he should have set up a separate trust for X. However, insofar as the deceased's duty was concerned, it seems to me that the trust arrangement should, all things being equal, have met and covered all the exigencies of this case, including the foreseeable difficulties X might later encounter."

III. INTESTACY

There are two forms of intestacy: total intestacy and partial intestacy. Total intestacy occurs where someone dies without having made a valid will. Partial intestacy occurs where someone has made a valid will, but it does not cover all the testator's property.

TOTAL INTESTACY: DISTRIBUTION OF ESTATE

Deciding how property should be distributed on intestacy is a two-stage process.

Stage 1

The first stage involves asking a series of questions, in descending order. If one of those questions is answered affirmatively, there is no need to go on to the next question.

- First, does the deceased have a spouse/civil partner and/or issue living? If so, distribution according to Class 1 rules.
- If not, does the deceased have parents living? If so, distribution according to Class 2 rules.
- If not, does the deceased have brothers and sisters, or children of brothers and sisters, living? If so, distribution according to Class 3 rules.
- If not, does the deceased have any next-of-kin (descendants from a common ancestor) living? If yes, distribution according to Class 4 rules.
- If not, the property goes to the State as ultimate intestate successor.

Stage 2

After it has been decided which of the above classes of rules are applicable, those rules are then applied.

Class 1 rules
These apply when there is a spouse or civil partner and/or issue living.

Dealing with spouses first, if there is both a spouse and issue, the spouse gets two-thirds of the estate and the issue gets one-third. The term "issue" includes all blood descendants and the method of distribution as between the issue is usually *per stirpes*. In other words, grandchildren of the deceased only take if their parent is dead, and the cumulative share of the children of a deceased descendant cannot exceed the share which their parent would have received had they been alive.

If there is a spouse, but no issue, the spouse gets the whole estate. If there is issue, but no spouse, the issue get the whole estate with distribution *per stirpes*.

As regards situations where the deceased is survived by a civil partner, rather than a spouse, s.73 of the 2010 Act provides that, as with spouses, a civil partner is entitled to 2/3 of the estate if there are surviving issue, or to all the estate if no issue survives.

However, s.73 also states that a child of the intestate can apply as against the civil partner for additional provision over and above the share they would otherwise be entitled to on intestacy and a court will make an order for such additional provision "only if [it] is of the opinion that it would be unjust not to make the order, after considering all the circumstances", including the provision made by the intestate for that child during the intestate's lifetime, the age and reasonable financial requirements of the child, the intestate's financial situation and the intestate's obligations to the civil partner.

Class 2 rules

These apply if there is no spouse/civil partner or issue of the deceased, but one or both of his parents are alive. In that case, the surviving parent(s) get the whole estate. If both parents are alive, the estate is divided equally between them. If only one parent is alive, they get the whole estate.

Class 3 rules

If there is no spouse/civil partner, issue or parents then this set of rules is applied. If all the siblings of the deceased are alive, they take equally. If some siblings are alive and some deceased then the respective shares of deceased siblings are divided among their children. If all the siblings are deceased, then their children take equally. However, grandchildren of the siblings cannot take anything under this set of rules; this is not *per stirpes* distribution, although it may at first glance resemble it.

Class 4 rules

If there is no spouse/civil partner, issue, parents or siblings/children of siblings then this set of rules applies. Are there next-of-kin?

Next-of-kin means descendants from a common ancestor, of the nearest degree available. The rules for ascertaining degrees of relationship are set out in s.71(2) of the 1965 Act.

Briefly summarised, grandparents are the closest next-of-kin. So, if any grandparents of the intestate are alive, they will take the property. If no grandparents are alive, the property is divided equally between the intestate's aunts and uncles. In the unlikely eventuality that there are no grandparents, aunts or uncles alive, but there is a great-grandparent alive, the great-grandparent will get the estate.

If there are no grandparents, great-grandparents, aunts or uncles, then the estate will be divided equally between such grand-aunts and uncles, first cousins and grand-nephews and uncles of the intestate as are alive. If none of the above are alive, then we must move on to first cousins once removed, second cousins and so on.

When applying the next-of-kin rules, it is therefore necessary to ask:

- Are there grandparents of the intestate alive? If not, ask;
- Are there aunts and/or uncles of the intestate alive? If not, ask;
- Are there great-grandparents of the intestate alive? If not, ask;
- Are there grand-nephews and nieces, grand-aunts or uncles, or first cousins of the intestate alive?

For the purposes of all the intestacy rules relatives of the half blood are treated in the same way as relatives of the full blood, and illegitimate children are treated in the same way as legitimate children. The 1965 Act specifically provides that adopted children are to be treated the same as natural children for the purposes of intestacy. If there are no next-of-kin available, the State takes as ultimate intestate successor.

INTESTACY: ADMINISTRATION OF ESTATE

Obviously the deceased will not have nominated anybody to act as executor, since there was no will. However, anybody who stands to benefit on intestacy may apply to the court to be granted letters of administration. Once the court has appointed administrators, they can apply for a grant of probate. Once this is granted, the property vests in them; prior to that it vests in the Master of the High Court. The administrator gathers in the assets and pays off the debts. As with executors under a will, an administrator on intestacy has the power to sell off part of the estate in order to pay debts, and also the power to appropriate part of the estate for a specific beneficiary. He must then distribute the estate to the persons entitled on intestacy. He must do this by making an assent.

It may be noted that an intestate's spouse/civil partner has no legal right share on a total intestacy. It is not necessary to give them this right because under the rules on intestacy they are entitled (subject in the case of a civil partner to the qualification set out above) to the whole estate if there are no issue, or two-thirds if there are issue. This is significantly greater than her legal right share.

Similarly, a child's right to make a section 117 application only applies when the deceased dies wholly or partially testate. It does not apply on a total intestacy.

IV. RIGHTS OF COHABITANTS

As stated above, the 2010 Act gives registered civil partners rights under s.111 and on intestacy. The definition of "civil partner" is confined to members of same-sex relationships who have registered their relationship as a civil partnership. Accordingly, these rights are not relevant to opposite-sex couples who are not married or indeed same-sex couples who have not registered their civil partnership.

However, s.194 of the 2010 Act makes alternative provision for cohabitants (defined as two adults of the same or the opposite sex who have lived together as a couple in an intimate and committed relationship for at least five years, or for at least two years if the parties have one or more dependent children). Under the 2010 Act, a cohabitant of a deceased has the right to apply to the court for provision from their estate within six months of the grant of representation in relation to the estate, whereupon the court may make such provision for the applicant as it considers appropriate "having regard to the rights of any other person having an interest in the matter, if the court is satisfied that proper provision in the circumstances was not made for the applicant during the lifetime of the deceased for any reason other than conduct by the applicant that, in the opinion of the court, it would in all the circumstances be unjust to disregard."

Where the relationship ended before the death of the deceased, s.194(5) provides that the right of the cohabitant to make such an application is excluded in most (but not absolutely all) cases.

Index

adverse possession, 1, 3, 23, 80, 81, 88–109
  estate of deceased, and, 107–109
  de facto ownership, 3
  defences, 101–103
    acknowledgement, 101, 102
    disability, 103
    fraud, 102, 103
  expiration period, 88, 89
  extinguishment of title, 103
    effect of, 103–105
      parliamentary conveyance, 104
      possessory title, 103, 104
  jus possidendi, 104
  leasehold land, and, 105–107
    stranger against tenant, 105, 106
    stranger against landlord, 106
    tenant against landlord, 106
    tenant against adjoining property owner, 107
  requirements for, 89–101
    animus possidendi, 23, 90, 92, 95, 97–99
    dispossession, 90, 91
    frustration of rightful owner, 99–101
    possession without permission, 96, 97
    squatter in possession, 92–95

base fee, 8, 9

civil partners, 1
  consent to sale, 84 *see also* **family home**
  intestacy, and, 129–131 *see also* **intestacy**

legal right share, 119–121
revocation of will, 114, *see also* **succession, wills**
statutory rights, 119
transfer of land, 83, 87
cohabitants, 1,
  proper provision, 132
  statutory rights, 119, *see also* **intestacy, succession**
  transfer of land, 83
co-ownership, 16–20
  determination of, 20
    partition, 20
    sale, 20
    union in a sole tenant, 20
  four unities, 16–17
    unity of interest, 16
    unity of possession, 16
    unity of time, 17
    unity of title, 16
  joint tenancy, 16–17, 18
    creation of, 18
    definition of, 16
    severance, 17, 19, 20
      words of, 18
      registration of judgment mortgage and, 19
      unilateral, 20
    survivorship, 16
  tenancy in common, 17, 18
    creation of, 18
    definition of, 18
covenants, 3, 13, 15 *see also* **freehold covenants**
  restrictive, 24, 34, 36, 37
conveyance, 75, 78, *see also* **transfer of land**
  civil partners and, 87
  definition of, 84
  family home and, 84–87

dispositions, 28, 84 *see also* **transfer of land**
testamentary, 110, 119, *see also* **succession, wills**
duress, 46, 68, 85

easements, 1, 2, 3, 21–30, 40, 42, 75, 76, 79, 80, 81, 82, 99, 104
  acquisition of, 25–30, 94
    express grant, by, 25
    express reservation, by, 25
    implied grant, by, 25, 27
    implied reservation, by, 25
    prescription, 28
      2009 Act regime, 29, 30
      lost modern grant, 29
      pre-2009 Act regime, 28, 29
  characteristics of, 21–25,
    dominant tenement, 21, 22, 24, 25–28
      benefit, the, 22, 24,
      right must be capable of forming subject matter of grant, 23, 24
    servient tenement, 21–25, 27–29
  common intention, 26
  definition of, 2, 21
  incorporeal hereditament, 21, 40, 79
  necessity, 29
  negative, 3
  positive, 2
  quasi, 27, 28
  Wheeldon v Burrows, rule in, 27, 28
equity, 1, 3–5, *see also* **mortgages, trusts**
  business, 61, 62
  definition of, 3
  equitable mortgages, 64, 65
    redemption, 65
  equitable estate, 5
  equitable interests, 4, 5
  equitable ownership, 5
  equity's darling, 4, 77
  freehold estates, in, 7
  improvement, 61
  interests in land, 4
  long user, 61
  mere equities, 4
  mortgages, intervention in relation to, 65
    right to redeem, 65
    equity of redemption, 65–69, 102
    scrutiny of terms, 66
  proprietary estoppel, 42, 43
  scheme of development, 37, 38
  Tulk v Moxhay, rule in 34–36
estate *pur autre vie*, *see* **freehold ownership**
estoppel, 4, 40–43, 75, 76, 84
  detrimental reliance, 42,43
  licence, 40–42
  proprietary estoppel, 40, 42, 43
    conditions, for, 42
  proprietary right, 40
  personal right, 40
  remedies for, 42,43

family home, 43, 75, 83–87
  civil partners, and, 83
  consent to sale of,
    dispensing of, 86
    exceptions to requirement of, 85
    civil partner, 84, 87
    prior, in writing, 84
    spouse, 84
  definition of, 84
  inter vivos transfer of, 75
  purchaser for full value of, 83
  spouses rights, 83
fee farm grants, *see* **freehold ownership**
fee tail, *see* **freehold ownership**
freehold covenants, 3, 31–39
  annexation, 36, 37
    statutory, 37
  assignment, 37
  benefit of, 31, 32
  breach of, 31
  burden of, 31, 32, 33
  covenantee, 31

covenantor, 31
enforcement of,
    against successor in title of
        covenantor, 33
    against successor in title of
        covenantor by successor in
        title of covenantee, 34–35
    enforcement of by successor in
        title of covenantee, 33
    pre-December 2009, 32–33
    post-December 2009, 32
extinguishment of, 38, 39
negative covenant, 34
personal to a party, 32
restrictive covenant, 24, 34, 36, 37
scheme of development, 37, 38
Tulk v Moxhay, rule in, 34–36
unreasonable interference, 39
unregistered land, 35
freehold ownership, 2, 6–12
hybrid interest, 13–15
    fee farm grants, 13, 14, 15, 81
    lease for lives, 13, 14
types of,
    estate *pur autre vie,* 5, 8, 9–12,
        103
        remainder, 9, 10
        reversion, 9, 10
        trustees of, 11
    fee simple, 6, 7
        modified, 6
        conditional, 6,7
        determinable, 6, 7
        impermissible restrictions, 7
    fee tail, 8,9, 103
        female, 8
        male, 8
    life estate, 2, 5, 9–12, 16, 33, 103
        trustees of, 11

incorporeal hereditaments, *see*
    easements
intestacy, 128–131, *see also*
    succession
adverse possession, and, 107, 108

joint tenancy, and, 16
    partial, 116, 128
    rights of cohabitants, 132
    rules of, 3, 75, 110
    total, 128
        administration of estate, 131
        distribution of estate, 129–131
imputed notice, 35, 77, 85

joint tenancy, *see* **co-ownership**

leasehold ownership, 1, 2, 13, 44–63
definition of, 2
forfeiture, 44
landlord-tenant relationship, 47–63
    creation of, 44–47
        agreement, 44
        agreement valid under
            contract law, 46
        necessary written
            requirements fulfilled, 46
    types of, 47, 48
        fixed term, 47
        periodic, 48
    non-residential tenancies,
        extent of rights, 62, 63
        obligations of landlords and
            tenants, 54–57
        statutory rights, 61, 62
        termination, 57–61
    residential tenancies, 48, 49
        obligations of landlords, 49, 50
        statutory rights of tenants under,
            50, 51
        termination, 51–54
leases, *see* **leasehold ownership**
leases for lives, *see* **freehold
    ownership**
licences, 40–42, *see also* **estoppel**
definition of, 40
licensee, 40
licensor, 40
personal right, 40
proprietary right, 40
types of, 40–42

licences *(continued)*
  proprietary right *(continued)*
    types of *(continued)*
      bare licence, 40, 41
      contractual, 41
      coupled with a proprietary
        interest, 40
      estoppel, 41 *see also* **estoppel**

misrepresentation, 4, 85,
mistake, 4, 46, 85, 111
mortgages, 64–74
  definition of, 64
  judgment mortgage, 74
  mortgagee, rights of, 69
    pre-2009 Act, under, 69, 70
      appoint receiver, 71
      possession, 70
      sale, 70, 71
    post-2009 Act, under, 72, 73
      appoint receiver, 73
      possession, 72, 73
      sale, 73
  mortgagor, rights of, 69
    redeem, 69
  types of,
    equitable, 64, 65, *see also* **equity**
    legal, 64

ownership, *see* **co-ownership,**
  freehold ownership, leasehold
  ownership

partition, 20,
perpetuities, rule against, 9
profit à prendre, 30, 76, 94, 98
proprietary estoppels, *see* **estoppel**
Purefoy v Rodgers, rule in, 9

registered land, 78, 79, *see also*
  leasehold ownership,
  unregistered land
  administration of registered title, 79,
    80
  actual occupation rights, 82, 83

class of title, 80
  absolute, 80
  good leasehold, 80
  possessory, 80
  qualified, 80
compulsory registration, 79
investigation of title of, 78–83
  identifying third party interests, 81
    overriding interests, 81, 82
    registrable burdens, 81
rectification of register, 82, 83
registration of title, *see* **registered**
  land, unregistered land

Settled Land Acts,
  estates *pur autre vie,* and, 10
  trusts, under, 11, *see also* **trusts**
  trustees of settlement, 11
succession, 110–132 *see also*
  intestacy, wills
  co-habitants, 131, 132
  intestacy, 128–131
  moral duty of testator, 121–128
  statutory rights of, 119–128
    civil partners, 119–121
    children, 121–128
    spouses, 119–121
  testate, 110–119

tenancy in common, *see* **co-ownership**
tenements, 55, 56, 61
transfer of land, 75–87, *also,*
  conveyance, intestacy,
  unregistered land
  conveyances, 75
  family home protection, 75
  inter vivos, 75
    words of limitation, 75
  on death, 75, *see also* **succession**
trusts,
  2009 Act regime, 10, 11, 12
  constructive, 5, 78
  dispute resolution, 12
  express, 5, 11
  implied, 5

resulting, 78
transfer of land, and, 75
Tulk v Moxhay, rule in, *see* **equity, freehold covenants**

undue influence, 4, 46, 68, 85
unregistered land, 76
   notice, doctrine of, 77
   investigation of title of, 76–78
      good root of title, 76
      identifying third party interests, 76
      purchaser without notice, equity's darling, 76
      registry of deeds, 77, 78

Wheeldon v Burrows, rule in, *see* **easements**
Whitby v Mitchell, rule in, 9
wills, 110–119, *see also* **succession**
   additions, 113, 114

administration, 114, 115
   grant of, 114, 115
   letters of, 115
   personal representatives, 115
capacity, 111
changes, 113, 114
definition of, 110
formal requirements, 111–113
   signed, 111, 112
   witnessed, 112, 113
   writing, 111
interpretation, 116
   armchair principle, 116, 117
   extrinsic evidence, 117–119
   speaks from death, 115, 116
moral duty, of testator, 121–128
revoking, 114
statutory rights, 119–128
   civil partners, 119–121
   children, 121–128
   spouses, 119–121